Breaking in the Back Door to the Ivy League

Marshall Lawrence Burstein, J.D.

Author

ISBN 978-0615704319

Foreword

I would like to dedicate this book to my father, Frank Burstein, and my mother, Denise Raidman Burstein, both of whom provided me with more than I could ever ask. Most of all, I would like to extend my many thanks to the staff and faculty who helped me during my tenure at Manor College, including Patti McEnery and Jane Zegestowsky, all of whom provided me with opportunities that have enabled me to get to where I am today.

Very truly yours,

Marshall Lawrence Burstein, J.D.

Table of Contents

Prologue

Now, I assume that you picked up this book because either you or someone you know desires to attain admission into an Ivy League university. Most people have aspirations. Some people first aspire to have a family while others yearn for academic excellence. Were your grades too low during high school? Was your standardized admission test score below par? You are not alone and by no means has the inability to acquire these credentials ruined your opportunity to achieve this goal. My own story reflects these insecurities, which, as one might think, are below the threshold for acquiring entrance into a prestigious university. It is for this reason that I am determined to provide you with an alternative route for maneuvering through the rigorous admissions process that accompanies an Ivy League education. As I reveal to you the process, I will provide you with my own story, and that of others, to assure you that it is possible to accomplish this same feat. This venture

1

requires neither legacy affiliation nor phenomenal athletic ability; only perseverance, ingenuity and dedication should be all you need to acquire admission. No longer will this goal be considered a pipe dream. Either you, or someone you know, can now achieve what others might think is unattainable.

To begin, I didn't have an all-star high school record. I graduated from high school with a 2.9 grade point average while ranking in the 50th percentile on the SAT despite my efforts to redeem myself after taking the exam twice. Additionally, my involvement in extra-curricular activities was minimal – I only participated in select choir. But even those involvements were nominal, as I rarely attended practices or performances. Looking back on it, I now realize why I rarely achieved any grade higher than a "C" in my high school chorus class. Oh yeah, I also only attended school as needed. When I did attend school, I felt the need to turn class time into nap time because I was on a block scheduling system, which requires students to sit in the classroom for one and a half hours per class.

The aforementioned information, however, doesn't tell you much about how I attained admission into one of the "Elite Eight," i.e., Cornell University. You can only see that the failure to have the credentials, which most believe are necessary to attain admission into a highly ranked university, will not bar a student from attaining entrance into his or her 'reach' school. However, the trick to following my advice is not only figuring out what you need to do but at what time you need to start performing at your maximum potential. Remember, turning your performance around 180 degrees is possible; I know, I did it. I not only attained admission into Cornell University but was accepted into The University of California at Berkeley as well as Tulane University in New Orleans. The admissions committee at Cornell University's School of Industrial and Labor Relations accepted sixty transfer credits, which meant I only had to complete two years at Cornell to receive my bachelor's degree. The admissions committee at The University of California at Berkeley waived academic requirements. Tulane University

3

provided me with scholarship money. And smaller institutions offered me nearly full tuition scholarships after only acquiring a measly financial burden at my initial undergraduate school, Manor College, in Jenkintown, Pennsylvania.

But how did I have access to these opportunities? You're probably asking yourself that very question at this moment; however, that's the question I seek to answer in the subsequent pages that follow while providing you with the information necessary to attain what I achieved. I plan to infuse the hope in your beliefs that either you, or someone you know, can accomplish what I accomplished. Remember, high school is not the only stepping stone for a student's academic success. With my advice, you can break in the back door and pay nearly half the price for the world's most elite education. It's worth a shot. What do you have to lose? Not a thing.

Chapter 1
Advantages to Breaking in the Back Door

You need to forget the stigma that is attached to attending a two-year college. There are many advantages to attending a two-year college prior to matriculating into a four-year institution. By attending a two-year college and transferring to a four-year school, you will enjoy benefits that most students entering a four-year college immediately after graduating high school miss out on. I have set forth below eight key advantages to why breaking in the back door to any four-year college or university is a business savvy decision.

1. You can acquire a four-year college degree for nearly half the price.

2. You will attain your bachelor's degree from the four-year institution where you eventually transfer.

3. Employers care more about where you acquire your bachelor's degree than your associate's degree.

4. Two-year colleges provide smaller classroom settings where you can much more easily excel academically, which will

5

enhance your overall GPA; this helps with graduate program applications.

5. Two-year colleges generally provide easier curriculums where you can easily adjust to the college academic environment.

6. Students who attend two-year colleges have scholarship opportunities when they transfer, which are unavailable to students who enroll in a four-year school traditionally.

7. After two years, you will receive an associate's degree that you will never lose, which is beneficial if you are unable to complete the four years required for your bachelor's degree.

8. Two-year colleges usually have agreements with four-year institutions, which enable students to easily transfer credits after attaining those credits at a cost-effective price.

Chapter 2
High School

In September 1999, I entered the halls of William Tennent High School in Warminster, Pennsylvania. As I walked down the long corridors, the halls seemed dark. Narrow lockers lined the walls, which patiently awaited the incoming class. I remember thinking how the building would be the bane of my very existence for the next four years. As the thought overcame me, I grew impatient. I could not wait until the day my years in school would end. Eighth grade seemed light years away even though ninth grade was just about to begin. I was about to start taking my core substantive courses but I didn't have the drive to achieve the grades I needed to gain admission into an elite university upon graduation. I just didn't care.

There it was. The first day, and I had already given up hope. I didn't have motivation; the ambition to achieve. I'm sure some students wanted to walk out senior year with perfect academic records; these students knew from the very beginning that they wanted to attain admission into prestigious colleges and universities while acquiring the most sought after high school academic credential: Valedictorian. But, as I remember it, my valedictorian never went to an Ivy League school. Of course, the school he attended was elite. But, was it an Ivy League university? No. To add insult to injury, my high school grades never mirrored my valedictorian's; however, I still managed to attain admission into a university, which prides itself in ranking higher than the university he attended as recognized by the U.S. News and World Report. Astounding, huh?

Nonetheless, I remember sitting through class during my first day of school. Classes started at 7:30 am. Unable to leave the academic building for fear of being truant, I sat in on every single class. The subject matter was dry and I was bored out of my mind. I stayed in the building until the school bell rang at 2:15 pm. As soon as that bell rang, I ran to the busses. After arriving home, I quickly threw off my schoolbag, grabbed the phone, made a call and headed right back out the way I came in. My parents beckoned: "Don't you have homework to do?" "No," I cried out as I forgot what homework my teachers assigned for the following day. My thoughts of school faded as I hurried down the road to entertain myself with my closest friends.

The entire year followed the same routine. I would wake up, go to school, return home, go out, and sleep. Nowhere in my hectic schedule did I have time to complete my schoolwork. I mean, how could I make the time? Other things were much more important. I spent weekend nights reminiscing with old friends while meeting new ones at underage nightclubs. I worried more about my next girlfriend than acing my next math examination. Therefore, I prioritized my time accordingly. I made sure to go out due to my undying need to have fun even though I knew my grades would suffer. However, I remember thinking that high school would never do anything for me. And, I assure you, I was right.

As for my academic curriculum, freshman year followed the normal scheme. My core classes consisted of Algebra, General Science, History, Music, and English. I did not have high grades. I achieved mostly C's. I remember, one day, sitting in the hallway before class, scrambling to cheat on a math take-home examination. I didn't have enough time to complete the test. Of course, I ended up receiving an "F" as my grade for the examination. Luckily, I passed the class.

Most students in my situation would have probably attempted to alter their performance half-way through freshman year but I didn't have my sights set on attending college. Grades meant nothing to me at the time. I learned just enough to pass. Every time I received a progress report my parents would inquire as to how I performed and I would lie to them and tell them that I achieved mostly A's and B's. By doing this, I was able to buy myself some time before they grounded me. Though, after a week of punishment, I would be back to hanging out with my closest companions. Performing well in high school, for me, was an utter joke.

My friendship circle during freshman year didn't help the situation either. Some friends were ok, but most were bad seeds. With their help I would find myself getting into mischief. For example, I remember running around during weekday nights outside the local convenience store. My friends and I would ask bystanders to purchase cigarettes for us with whatever money we could scrounge. We would then create elaborate plans where the people who purchased our cigarettes could hide the cigarettes they just purchased so we could pick the packs up without suspicion; this was my life freshman year. The blinders were on. My friends didn't help.

My sophomore year was nothing to brag about either. Sure, I was chosen for my high school's select choir; however, I began cutting class and missing school. I was no longer afraid of being truant. I figured if I was caught, I would make up a convincing lie, which would enable me to escape suspension. For instance,

I remember cutting class one day during sophomore year. As I was walking down the street near my home, the Academic Dean drove past me. He asked me why I was walking the streets during the school day. Of course, I wasn't going to tell him the truth so I lied to him and told him that I was on my way to a friend's house to pick up medication because I was sick. He told me that he was going to call my parents as soon as he returned to the school. Realizing that my parents had no idea that I was playing hooky, I showed up to school just in time for lunch. In the cafeteria, the Academic Dean gave me a puzzled look, probably realizing that I only showed up to school because I didn't have a valid excuse to miss class. Luckily, the Academic Dean never called my parents.

Although you might be thinking to yourself that most kids play hooky once in a while, I will assure you that my fun didn't stop there. Not only did I cut class without permission, but I also wrote my own early dismissal notes. However, I was not alone because some of my high school friends were exactly the same. Most of them had no desire to perform well academically even though they had a lot of potential; they cut class and wrote their own early dismissal notes too.

I did, however, begin spending less time with my high school friends and more time with my high school girlfriend. Now, I've only brought up my high school girlfriend to reveal to you the distractions that I encountered while enrolled in high school. Let's call my high school girlfriend, "Stacey." I met Stacey while I was at the beach during summer vacation just before entering my sophomore year. Although the relationship eventually dissipated, I spent the weekends during my sophomore year hitching rides to visit her. She lived over an hour away. My best friend at the time was dating her best friend, so he and I would strategically car pool half-way only to have someone else's parent pick us up for an entire weekend. My parents really didn't approve but I didn't care. The more time I spent with Stacey, the more my focus in school diminished. I remember cutting class to hang out with Stacey when I was scheduled to take a Spanish examination. I didn't study, so of course I didn't feel like taking the test. But, when the teacher decided to allow me to retake the examination, I skipped the re-scheduled test to hang out with Stacey again. To make a long story short, I ended up with a "D" in the class. But who's to blame me? I was enjoying my time and I was still passing.

Junior year came and went just as quickly as the previous two years. However, this year, something was different. I no longer had the same friends. Most of my high school friends moved on to other schools. And some could no longer attend William Tennent because they got sent to the district's satellite school for juveniles. Luckily, I didn't end up in either one of those situations. Nonetheless, just as I entered junior year, Stacey moved in with me. You might be asking yourself how I was able to convince my parents to let Stacey move in with us. Well, that took some advocacy on my part. I told my parents that I would drop out of school if they did not allow her to move in. I must have spent a few weeks attempting to convince them to allow her to stay. Eventually, with enough persistence, my parents caved. Now, I'm sure you're all thinking that my parents were crazy. Maybe they were. But, hey, at least I got what I wanted.

I was in my own world. My clique was gone. Some of my high school friends got wrapped up into hard drugs. But I wasn't hanging out with them when they ventured down that path because they moved on to other schools in different areas. Since I could no longer find refuge in my old clique, I found myself attempting to alter my academic performance. I started trying; however, the attempts failed. Such stretches did not last very long. I didn't have anything motivating me to perform well in school. I lived with Stacey. I went out whenever I wanted. During junior year, I just existed. I had no goals, no direction.

Finally, senior year was upon me. As my high school education was coming to an end, I began to wonder whether I would ever become successful. Though, I'm not sure if I was really certain what "success" meant at that moment. I believed, however, that I could become successful if I performed well academically during senior year. I didn't realize that I was about to start running a sprint in a long-marathon that I would never be able to win. I mean, how could I catch up to those students who had been running the entire time? The students who had their hopes set on becoming valedictorian from the first day of high school were the ones who were meant to win the race. The feeling was comparable to cramming for an exam that you didn't study for all semester. After realizing that you couldn't possibly understand the information as well as others who spent the whole semester preparing, it no longer seems worthwhile to even bother trying to perform well.

From the outset, I wasn't sure what I wanted to become or what I wanted to do in life. It wasn't until I was about to graduate high school that I even realized that I didn't have the tools to enter a lucrative profession. Who knew that you needed to have strong academic credentials to become a doctor or a lawyer? Can you say ignorance? I knew my only options were private two-year colleges, state-school satellite campuses, and community colleges. For this reason, I didn't put much effort into deciding where to attend school. I didn't research any colleges or universities. I didn't know which four-year universities I would transfer to upon completing my degree. Heck, I didn't even know that transferring to a four-year school was an option. However, I knew that at some point, I wanted to graduate with at least a bachelor's degree. I didn't want to settle for a career. I wanted to make my career. Nonetheless, I didn't know how to get there. For these reasons, I allowed my parents to decide what school I should initially attend. My parents decided that I should attend a private two-year college, which would provide me with a liberal arts education as well a vocational associate's degree. Four years in high school provided me with the foundation to become a working class citizen, punching in nine-to-five, struggling to stay above the poverty line. An associate's degree would give me something more.

Although I wasn't sure what route to take or how to circumvent the routine admissions process for gaining admission into a four-year college, I recognize now that if I had known some tricks and had access to the right resources, my anxiety would have probably been much lower when I graduated high school. For this reason, I am going to outline for you the steps that I took, which landed me into one of the nation's most prestigious institutions. Remember, the only thing a high school record reveals to the "Elite" universities is whether a student can perform. Once I demonstrated that I could perform, even after I graduated high school, my high school record was discarded. The SAT was given less weight. Of course, Cornell University did it for me. The Ivy League universities, or any other school for that matter, should do it for you.

Chapter 3
Start Knockin':
Things to Consider Before Applying

Most students have no idea where to start as they begin the transfer admissions process. In my opinion, you should start knockin' well before you start applying to schools for transfer admission. It is much easier to transfer to a four-year institution if you start preparing prior to enrolling at your initial undergraduate institution; however, extensive early preparation is not entirely necessary. For this reason, I have set forth a five-tip list below, which you should keep in mind as you navigate through the transfer application process for any institution.

1. Take the SAT or ACT

Although this seems blatantly obvious, you should take the SAT or ACT before you enroll in any college. Some colleges or universities do not require the SAT or ACT. Although most colleges and universities do not give the SAT or ACT much, or any, weight during the transfer application process, most schools require the SAT or ACT for transfer admission. Even if you're lucky enough to find a school that does not require the SAT or ACT, you will increase your odds at getting into the school of your choice by making it a point to take the examination. You do not want to waste your time sitting through the SAT or ACT during your sophomore year in college to get into a school for transfer admission. Take the test even if you believe you will not perform well on the exam. During the transfer process, college admissions counselors are more interested in college performance rather than standardized test scores. To find out more about the SAT or ACT, you can spend your time browsing www.collegeboard.com.

2. <u>Assess Costs at Two-Year & Four-Year Schools</u>

You should know that the cost of a four-year college degree can be extraordinarily high especially if you enroll at a private college or university. For this reason, you might be better off attending your local community college for a few thousand dollars per year as opposed to attending a four-year college right away. And because tuition at Ivy League universities is particularly high, it is especially important to keep your costs down while attending your initial undergraduate institution if an Ivy League school is your ultimate goal. Remember, you're only going to be transferring the credit. You're not buying the degree. However, four-year schools that are willing to provide you with partial or full tuition scholarships are worth looking into for freshman admission. As a general principle, you should keep the cost of your first two years at a minimum.

3. <u>Assess Leadership Opportunities</u>

When you begin looking into what schools you want to attend during your first two years of college, you are better off finding an institution that will provide you with leadership opportunities. Leadership roles are invaluable because they demonstrate to admissions committee members that you can accomplish tasks without supervision. Most Ivy League university admissions counselors admit students who have served in some type of leadership capacity. Because such positions can add value to your transfer application, you should assess the leadership opportunities that are available at the two-year or four-year colleges where you might first enroll. You're better off at a school where you can acquire such a spot. Holding a leadership position will make your transfer application stand out above other applicants.

4. <u>Draft a List of Potential Four-Year Schools</u>

Although you might think it is too early to draft a complete list of schools to which you hope to transfer, it is never too early to begin brainstorming where you want to attend to attain your bachelor's degree. You should write out a list of schools where you would like to transfer. Even if you don't draft a complete list of potential transfer-to schools right away, you will need to keep in mind what schools you want to attend because you will need to complete transfer requirements for each school prior to enrollment; these requirements are likely different for each institution. Incorporate a few safety schools.

If you are going to be attending a two-year college, look into four-year colleges that have dual admissions or articulation agreements with the two-year college that you are going to attend. Dual admissions agreements are agreements between two-year colleges and four-year institutions; these agreements enable students to transfer to select schools as juniors with all the credits they earned while attending a particular two-year college. Articulation agreements are comparable to dual admissions agreements but are generally not as favorable. Students who transfer through articulation agreements may have some but not all of their credits transfer to their new institution. If you attend a two-year college, the transfer counselors will have these agreements at their disposal. You need to ensure that you are on your way to securing a bachelor's degree using the most cost-effective approach regardless of the four-year school where you eventually hope to graduate.

5. Research Transfer Requirements

At some point during the first two years of your undergraduate education, you will need to research what course requirements you must fulfill to transfer to the school of your choice. Throughout the transfer process, you should collect information on what educational requirements each school requires to ensure that you are taking the courses required for transfer admission. Different schools have different requirements. Although some schools might waive transfer requirements, you will make yourself a more competitive applicant if you can fulfill the course requirements that each institution desires. Even if a particular college or university only prefers that prospective applicants take certain courses, you should make sure to take those classes because it will provide you with an advantage over those students who have not taken those courses. For your convenience, I have published an appendix in the back of this book, which includes requirements for transfer admission to each Ivy League school.

Chapter 4
"Trigger Moment"

Now, once I started performing well in college many people started asking me the same question: "What triggered your desire to perform well academically?" I generally get this question from parents and guidance counselors; however, sometimes students ask me why I altered my academic performance after I failed to try for so many years. I imagine that people think I had a "Trigger Moment." I, however, don't think that this moment occurred. For me, I can't pinpoint the exact minute, the exact phrase, or the exact event. I'm sure if I attempted to boil it down to the precise moment in milliseconds the incident that triggered my desire to spend so many countless nights making note cards would be too hard to uncover. However, I can tell you that I do know the exact reasons why I chose to perform well enough during my time at Manor College, which gave me the tools I needed to catapult myself into an Ivy League university.

My reasons equate to what most people would believe is a "Trigger Moment." Nonetheless, my decision making process is probably better off being called "Trigger Reasoning." My reasoning was basic goals, which I formulated for myself during my senior year of high school. I no longer wanted to be an underachiever at life.

Underachievers exist. Many students perform well below their potential. As I can only tell you about my own performance or lack thereof, I can advise you that I didn't perform well because I chose not to perform well. Doing well academically took energy; this was energy I wasn't willing to exert toward my studies. As I've mentioned previously, many other things were much more important so I prioritized accordingly. However, I began to recognize that in order to achieve my goals I would have to make academics my top priority. By making my academics a priority, I began to see academic performance as a means to an end rather than the end itself. I didn't realize that performing well academically would make it much easier for me to excel in the real-world until I reached my senior year in high school. I didn't know that having a degree from an established and nationally recognized four-year institution could provide me with opportunities much more lavish than I would be able to attain with either an associate's or bachelor's degree from a less recognized institution. The alumni connections. The pedigree. The ease to which I could attain admission into a graduate school or obtain a well paying job. Furthermore, the lucrative profession I strived to enter essentially required both a bachelor's and graduate degree from nationally recognized institutions.

When I graduated high school, I decided that I wanted to become a lawyer. There were a few reasons why I chose to work toward attaining a law degree. For one, I wanted the social recognition. I never had credentials which others sought. For this reason, I felt as though having the degree would make others admire me. I also wanted the opportunity to enter a profession where I could earn a salary well above the poverty line. I wanted a career which would challenge me intellectually. I also felt that if I pursued a career as an attorney I would be able to capitalize on my talents as well as my credentials to become an entrepreneur. I remember watching my brother's friends struggling to make a living and unable to move out while in their late twenties. I didn't want to end up like that. I wanted more out of life. I wanted the "American Dream."

Nonetheless, I recognized that I would eventually have to enroll at a four-year college or university in order to achieve my long-term career goals. I also knew that I had to perform well during my time in college to gain access to a decent law school. My drive to become a lawyer motivated me to excel in college. I had a goal in mind, which is why I decided to exert my energy into performing well in school. It wasn't my short term goal of getting into an elite institution but rather a battle plan for securing a job in the career of my choice. Without a long-term goal, I never would have had the desire to perform well in college. However, I recognized that it wasn't too late to set my sights on a goal. Although there were times where I would get discouraged, I would think of those eighty-year olds who crafted bucket lists in hopes of completing every task before they died. With a goal in mind, it was much easier for me to use the resources, which were available to me, to excel in most everything in which I participated.

As a general rule, goals will motivate you to perform well academically. You must recognize that having a goal is vital to performing well in school. Even if you have no direction, you should formulate a goal, which you currently want to achieve. Although the goal might change, the earlier you set your sights on a goal the easier it will be for you to stay on track from the very beginning of your college career. In either developing, or helping someone develop a goal, I have set forth a list of professions, which either require a college degree or where a college degree is vital for advancement. You will be much more inclined to put forth greater effort into your academic studies if you realize that you need a college degree with a stellar GPA to achieve your goal.

Remember, it's never too late to start. And, if you formulate a goal after sabotaging your high school record, there is still hope. If you put your energy into performing well during your tenure at a two-year college or during the first two years at a four-year institution, you can succeed in gaining admittance into an elite college or university. Remember, the bachelor's degree you eventually acquire will be yours forever. The better the school, the more marketable you will be. You will be more likely to obtain a coveted position in the field of your choice if you have highly sought after academic credentials from an elite institution. Furthermore, if you perform well academically prior to transferring to a four-year college, you will most likely save money no matter what school you transfer to upon completing your first two years, because better academic performance means more scholarship opportunities.

Human Resources Professional

Lawyer   Judge

Doctor of Osteopathic Medicine

I have set forth, below, a list of career choices to allow you to begin brainstorming whether your dream job requires a college degree. I have included average salary ranges to give you a general idea about how much money you would earn while working in each profession.[1]

1. Accountant – $37,551 - $51,193
2. Chiropractor – $42,014 - $77,819
3. Doctor - Neurologist – $118,905 - $203,566
4. Human Resources Director – $59,219 - $99,200
5. Judge, U.S. District Court – $80,000 - $122,443
6. Lawyer – $56,994 - $106,086
7. Mechanical Engineer – $52,846 - $71,621
8. Pharmacist – $75,718 - $104,096
9. Physical Therapist – $55,119 - $70,180
10. Physicist – $59,878 - $109,931
11. Professor – $57,458 - $103,594
12. Psychologist – $44,249 - $70,643
13. Registered Nurse – $45,926 - $63,980
14. Social Worker – $29,091 - $40,703
15. Speech Pathologist – $40,825 - $77,391

---

[1] www.payscale.com

If you can envision yourself working in any of the above-mentioned jobs, you should remember that nearly every person who works in these professions holds a college degree. Having a degree from an Ivy League university will make you look more appealing to prospective employers. If you're going to put your energy into attaining a degree to achieve your dream job, you might as well get the best degree your money can buy. Private four-year institutions, which are not as notable as Ivy League schools are comparable in cost; though, opportunities and alumni connections from Ivy League institutions can be much more valuable. Moreover, if you choose to attend a two-year college first and then transfer to a four-year college, regardless of the school, then you can reduce the total amount you borrow in student loans thereby increasing your disposable income after graduation. Performing well during your first two years in college, whether at a two-year or four-year school, will give you a chance to excel in the professional world even if you did not do so during high school.

Many people do not realize that having a goal in mind will make them more apt to perform at their maximum potential. Although I recognized that I had to sacrifice social time to work toward attaining my goal, I knew that the few years I spent in college were minimal compared to the amount of time I would be working in the professional world. For this reason, establishing a goal and putting forth effort to work toward achieving that goal was worthwhile.

Chapter 5
Eight Advantages to the Elite Eight

There are many advantages to acquiring a bachelor's degree from an Ivy League institution as opposed to other accredited colleges and universities. Although Ivy League graduates acquire degrees to work in the same industries as graduates from other colleges and universities, Ivy League schools are known for educating students who become some of the most notable and affluent. As there are too many reasons to list, I will provide you with eight advantages to attending one of the "Elite Eight" Ivy League schools.

1. Alumni Connections

The Ivy League universities provide an invaluable networking community that students have access to indefinitely. Because people who graduate from Ivy League universities work in a multitude of professions, you are likely to encounter an Ivy League graduate in any occupation you enter after graduation. Furthermore, certain corporations recruit Ivy League students just like professional sports teams proactively seek out athletes from Division I universities. Not only are alumni connections important for securing your first job, but they can also help when you are attempting to adjust to a new community or acquiring a degree from a graduate school. Alumni connections will come in handy even if you acquire a graduate degree from a different institution.

The Ivy League alumni associations have a vast array of resources, which are available to graduates. The associations distribute alumni magazines. They also sponsor clubs, which are active in various regions through the country; these clubs provide an opportunity for Ivy League graduates to network with one another. Each institution has an alumni networking website, which is available to graduates; the websites are listed on the next page.

> "The Ivy League Alumni Associations are invaluable networking resources."

Alumni Directories

Brown University	*www.alumni.brown.edu*
Columbia University	*www.columbia.edu/home/alumni/index.html*
Cornell University	*www.alumni.cornell.edu*
Dartmouth College	*www.alumni.dartmouth.edu*
Harvard University	*www.alumni.harvard.edu*
Princeton University	*www.alumni.princeton.edu*
University of Pennsylvania	*www.alumni.upenn.edu*
Yale University	*www.aya.yale.edu*

Specialized College Alumni Websites

Columbia University

Columbia University - School of General Studies
http://www.gs.columbia.edu/alumni

Cornell University

Cornell University - College of Agricultural & Life Sciences
http://www.cals.cornell.edu/cals/alumni-friends/index.cfm
Cornell University - College of Architecture, Art, & Planning
http://aap.cornell.edu/alumni
Cornell University - College of Arts & Sciences
http://as.cornell.edu/alumni
Cornell University - College of Engineering
http://www.engineering.cornell.edu/alumni-parents-friends/index.cfm
Cornell University - School of Hotel Administration
www.hotelschool.cornell.edu/alumni
Cornell University - School of Industrial & Labor Relations
www.ilr.cornell.edu/alumni/alumniassociation
Cornell University - School of Human Ecology
http://www.human.cornell.edu/che/alumni

University of Pennsylvania

University of Pennsylvania - Wharton School of Business
www.whartonconnect.com
University of Pennsylvania - Annenberg School of Communications
http://www.asc.upenn.edu/alumni

University of Pennsylvania - School of Arts & Sciences

http://www.sas.upenn.edu/home/views/alumni.html

University of Pennsylvania - School of Design

http://www.design.upenn.edu/alumniae

University of Pennsylvania - School of Engineering & Applied Science

http://www.seas.upenn.edu/alumni

University of Pennsylvania - School of Nursing

http://www.nursing.upenn.edu/alumni/Pages/default.asp

Notable Alumni

Brown - Scott Aversano (President of MTV Films), Walter Hoving (Former CEO of Tiffany & Co.), Lee Eliot Berk (President - Berklee College of Music)

Columbia - Robert Kraft (Owner of New England Patriots), Larry Grossman (Former CEO of NBC)

Cornell - Bill Nye (Scientist), Bill Maher (Political Satirist), Christopher Reeves (Actor), Paul Wolfowitz (President of the World Bank)

Dartmouth - Karl Barry Sharpless (2001 Nobel Prize - Chemistry), Dan Milisavljevic (Astronomer)

Harvard - Al Gore (Former U.S. Vice President), George W. Bush (Former U.S. President), Tommy Lee Jones (Actor)

Princeton - Jeff Bezos (Amazon.com Founder)

University of Pennsylvania - Jerome Allen (NBA Player), Richard Bloch (Co-Founder - H & R Block)

Yale - Bill Clinton (Former President), Meryl Streep (Actress), Henry Luce (Time Magazine Co-Founder), Sonia Sotomayor (U.S. Supreme Court Justice), Eli Whitney (Inventor)

2. Endowment, Scholarships, and Financial Aid

Ivy League institutions are known for their excessively large endowments. For example, Harvard University's endowment in 2011 was $31.728 billion. Endowments enable schools to provide incoming students with scholarship opportunities. Although the Ivy League schools do not generally provide merit-based scholarships to transfer students, the schools are known for their generous financial aid packages. Some schools, including Harvard and Yale, do not require students to take out loans to subsidize the cost of their undergraduate education, after a minimal student contribution, if the student's parents make below a certain income level. Without endowments, schools generally cannot afford to provide incoming students with these opportunities.

Nonetheless, the Ivy League schools may award transfer applicants merit-based scholarships after the students complete at least one semester at the institution. For example, Cornell University awarded me a merit-based scholarship after my first year. I never applied for the scholarship. My professors nominated me for the award. As a side note, certain outside organizations provide students who attend two-year colleges with scholarship opportunities, which pay for the student to finish a bachelor's degree at a four-year institution. Most notable is the Jack Kent Cooke Foundation, which offers a $30,000 per year scholarship for students to complete their education at the school of their choice. If you believe that the university where you wish to transfer does not provide sufficient financial aid or scholarship opportunities, you should look into outside scholarships while still attempting to transfer to the school of your choice.

Despite scholarships and financial aid, some Ivy League colleges are cheaper than other private four-year institutions because funding is not only derived from private resources but also from the state. For example, three undergraduate colleges at Cornell University are state land grant institutions; these colleges are the College of Agricultural and Life Sciences, the

College of Human Ecology, and the School of Industrial and Labor Relations. For this reason, New York state residents can enroll at certain colleges within Cornell University while paying nearly half-tuition each year. If you're a New York State resident, you can save money by attending one of these three schools rather than the other four colleges that makeup Cornell's entire undergraduate campus. And, if you're following my advice and attempting to break in through the back door, you should have already purchased your credits for a discount at your initial two-year or four-year school.

Endowment Funds[2]

Brown – $2.497 Billion (2011)
Columbia – $7.79 Billion (2011)
Cornell – $5.059 Billion (2011)
Dartmouth – $3.413 Billion (2011)
Harvard – $31.728 Billion (2011)
Princeton – $17.11 Billion (2011)
University of Pennsylvania – $6.582 Billion (2011)
Yale – $19.374 Billion (2011)

---

[2] http://www.nacubo.org/

3. <u>Notable Faculty</u>

The faculty employed at Ivy League institutions gives you yet another reason why attending an Ivy League school is superior to attending any other college or university. The professors who teach at these institutions are some of the most influential in their fields. Not only do the faculty members acquire their degrees from nationally recognized institutions, including Ivy League schools, but most have published books and articles in areas that they are now teaching. Many faculty members have also won awards in their fields of expertise. I have included on the next page, the number of Nobel Laureates who worked at each institution either during, before, or after they received the award.

Nobel Prizes are given out annually to individuals and organizations who excel in Chemistry, Physics, Literature, Peace, Physiology, or Medicine.

Nobel Laureates

(Faculty working after receipt of Nobel Prize)[3]

<u>Brown</u> - 1

<u>Columbia</u> - 9

<u>Cornell</u> - 6

<u>Harvard</u> - 1

<u>University of Pennsylvania</u> - 5

<u>Yale</u> - 2

Nobel Laureates

(Faculty who worked before or during receipt of Nobel Prize)

<u>Brown</u> - 2

<u>Columbia</u> - 58

<u>Cornell</u> - 22

<u>Harvard</u> - 38

<u>University of Pennsylvania</u> - 12

<u>Yale</u> - 23

Such credentials reveal that professors at Ivy League institutions are notable in their particular fields of study. Therefore, you will have the opportunity to learn from extremely intelligent educators. Moreover, most professors at the Ivy

---

[3] www.wikipedia.org (information updated as of 2010)

League schools are required to publish literature, books and articles. Of course, I was required to read some of my professors' materials as part of the course curriculum while enrolled at Cornell.

Additionally, faculty members at Ivy League schools are some of the most notable because they conduct a lot of research. For this reason, students who attend these institutions have excellent research opportunities; this makes Ivy League schools even more advantageous.

4. <u>Course Breadth</u>

Ivy League universities provide students with opportunities to take lots of different courses; this gives students the chance to achieve a very broad academic foundation. The Ivy League universities have many discipline areas, which include several individualized schools. Multiple disciplines provide unique opportunities for study. For example, Cornell University's School of Hotel Administration offers a course called Introduction to Casino Operations. Though, if witchcraft is your thing, Harvard College offers a course in Folklore and Mythology called Witchcraft and Charm Magic. Such courses provide students with a centralized focus in a particular area of study. Most four-year colleges and universities do not offer these types of courses, which informs you as to yet another reason why you might want to attend an Ivy League institution. For more information on course offerings, you can visit each institution's website.

5. <u>Diversity and Multi-Culturalism</u>

While in attendance at an Ivy League university, most students will be exposed to students from a diverse array of cultures and backgrounds; this diversity stems from both socio-economic and ethnic differences. Admissions counselors strive to admit students who can bring something different to the learning environment so academic discussion is far more stimulating than at most other schools. Ivy League students can also find other students who identify with their own racial, ethnic, or religious groups because of the diverse student bodies.

The multi-cultural environment also provides an opportunity for students to educate each other both academically and socially.

The Ivy League academic climate also fosters a culture of competition, which leads to more focused and disciplined students. Such an opportunity, although overwhelming at first, provides students with a foundation, which will help them while pursuing either a career or graduate school after graduation. The environment provides for a more active and engaging student body, which allows for lively classroom discussion. For this reason, cultural diversity and sensitivity is both fostered as well as created at Ivy League institutions.

6. <u>Career Advancement and Graduate School</u>

Students who receive Ivy League degrees are likely to have more opportunities for career advancement than students who do not attend such schools. Certain companies in different industries seek out workers who graduate from Ivy League schools especially for corporate executive level positions. Additionally, if a student moves across the country, human resource recruiters will recognize that the student received a phenomenal education. Most employers know each Ivy League school by name. If you attend a less prestigious institution, you could lose out on a job opportunity to someone who either attended an Ivy League school or a school in the recruiter's local geographic area due to your degree's lack of name recognition. You should want every advantage.

Attending an Ivy League undergraduate school can also help students attain admission into graduate school. While applying to graduate school, an Ivy League degree can help a student with a low standardized test score on a graduate entrance examination secure a spot at an outstanding institution. Graduate school administrators are more likely to hedge their bets on admitting an Ivy League graduate as opposed to a student from a less notable institution with the same major and GPA because students who attend Ivy League schools are known for performing well academically, as well as putting lots of time and energy into their studies.

7. Extra-Curricular Activities and Greek Life

Ivy League institutions are also well known for having lots of different extra-curricular organizations. Because these schools have been around for centuries, it is easy to understand why there are so many opportunities to participate in social activities on campus. Haven't you ever heard of Yale's Skull and Bones Society? The Ivy League schools esteemed societies include not only honor, but secret societies as well. Talk about elitism, huh? The Ivy League universities also provide "Greek Life" opportunities. The houses where the fraternities and sororities reside are lavish with exceptional architecture because "Greek Life" systems at Ivy League institutions are practically ancient; this truly provides students with an amazing social experience to supplement their academics. It is for these reasons that Ivy League universities provide some of the best extra-curricular and social opportunities that students will not find elsewhere.

8. Name Recognition

On a final note, name recognition is another advantage to attending an Ivy League institution. When a student attends an Ivy League institution, the brand name provides the student with prestige and social recognition. A lot of people think that our society deems those students who attend such institutions in the upper echelon of society. Even though this generalization is a stereotype, there is some truth that only those who are fortunate enough have access to such an education. Accomplishing what others think is almost nearly unattainable provides students with added value, which they will carry with them for the rest of their lives. The name recognition provides students with added value that employers' recognize. Moreover, attending such an institution provides students with increasing self-worth. While walking around an Ivy League campus, a student gets a positive feeling that he or she has accomplished what only few have achieved. Only a select few have the opportunity to attend an Ivy League university.

Chapter 6
Application Process: Post High School

The transfer admissions process starts right now. I will attempt to give you some insight into the steps that you need to take to secure a seat at an Ivy League university, especially if you graduate high school without the "right" credentials. If you are currently enrolled in college but still wish to transfer to an Ivy League university, you can either bypass this section or apply the following steps to the remainder of your time at your current institution. And just remember, you can follow my advice to break in the back door to any institution.

Now, if you're like most high school students who want to advance in today's society, you've probably spent time researching schools in order to figure out where you want to earn your bachelor's degree. I can tell you, however, that I was not one of those students. I was the student who stared awkwardly in the cafeteria at college sweatshirts because I didn't realize that there was such a variety of schools in the United

States. You could have asked me whether Cornell University was an Ivy League university and I would have honestly replied, "I have no idea." The only school I applied to following graduation was Manor College.

It wasn't until I immersed myself in my education at Manor College that I began to look into what other colleges and universities had to offer. It is for this reason that I am going to make this section short and sweet. Though, I will tell you that my tips on what you should do immediately upon graduating high school, will give you a jump start on pursuing your bachelor's degree from the university of your choice at the most cost-effective price.

For starters, if you have yet to enroll in college, you should look into two-year institutions; these include both public and private two-year colleges such as junior and community colleges. Elite universities are known to take students from two-year colleges either before or after such students have acquired an associate's degree. For example, Yale University's admissions website proclaims that, "Students may transfer from private or public colleges, and two or four-year institutions, though the Admissions Committee does give special consideration to those transfer candidates with community college experience... ." This just goes to show you that some prestigious universities actually prefer applicants who attended community colleges when assessing what students to accept for transfer admission.

"Students may transfer from private or public colleges, and two or four-year institutions, though the Admissions Committee does give special consideration to those transfer candidates with community college experience or military service."

- Yale University Website

Students who attend two-year colleges generally spend less money on a bachelor's degree because they do not shell out lots of money to attend school during the first two years while they are enrolled in college. And, they still end up acquiring the same bachelor's degree as the students who pay to go to the same school for all four years. Therefore, students who attend two-year colleges or four-year institutions on scholarship prior to enrolling in the four-year institutions from which they hope to graduate, can acquire bachelors' degrees for nearly half the price than what traditional students pay for the same college degree.

Furthermore, many people would probably agree that it is better to be a big fish in a small pond than a small fish in a huge lake. Two-year colleges can provide this advantage. For example, two-year colleges enable students to more easily acquire leadership positions. Most admission counselors would probably agree that students do not have enough time to build an extra-curricular resume before they transfer; however, the smaller pool of students in attendance at a two-year college creates an excellent opportunity to acquire a leadership position in a student activity group on campus. If you did not take on leadership roles in high school, this would be an appropriate time to start. Transfer admissions counselors look highly upon leadership credentials.

It's also important to remember that students enrolled in two-year colleges are often less competitive, which provides an opportunity for students to perform better academically than their peers. When striving to attain great grades, it is logically easier to obtain such credentials when competing against a less competitive student especially in a class where the teacher decides to curve the grading system. Also, because most students work hard during high school, they may get lazy when they start college. A two-year school will provide you with the chance to more easily outperform your peers while at the same time providing you with a chance at getting into the four-year school of your choice, even if you didn't have the right credentials when you graduated high school. Remember, high school is over. Now, an applicant's undergraduate GPA is what matters. Hear that? You can throw away that high school transcript. Students attempting to transfer only need to focus on what they can do to earn a spot at an Ivy League institution, or the school of their choice, as opposed to how they performed in high school.

At some point, you will need to pick out the school where you want to earn your bachelor's degree; otherwise, the energy you put into acquiring leadership positions and performing well academically will not be used for its most extreme potential. This task, however, does not have to be completed until you are well into your first year at your initial undergraduate institution. Nonetheless, you might want to get a head start because most colleges and universities, especially the Ivies, impose heavy restrictions on transfer students. Even if you have tediously researched schools while applying during your senior year of high school or you have no idea where *you would like to transfer, you will need resources crafted to fit the transfer admissions process. Do not get discouraged if you have already started your college education and have not yet researched schools for transfer admission. You are not likely behind! Remember, I am providing you with the information that I wish I knew. I did not start researching schools until my second semester in college. I never even heard of Cornell University until I completed my freshman year at Manor College.*

One of my goals right now is to reveal to you that each "Elite" educational institution has prerequisites that you must satisfy prior to enrolling as a transfer student. I didn't know this prior to enrolling at Manor College. I had limited time to figure out what academic credentials each school required transfer students to complete before matriculation. The transfer admissions process would have gone more smoothly if I discovered this information earlier on.

Some schools may waive transfer requirements. However, students should make sure that they tailor their academic course load to closely fit the school's basic transfer requirements; this will ensure that the application is at its strongest when applying. If a student completes the school's basic transfer requirements as well as the school's preferences for transfer admission, the student will have a better shot at getting in as a transfer student. For example, if the student's dream school is Harvard, then he/she should make sure that he/she doesn't attend a professional or vocational school. Harvard University is interested in ensuring that their transfer students have acquired a broad liberal arts background prior to matriculation.

But, don't sweat it if you're already enrolled in college and have begun to take courses in a particular field of study that is vocational in nature, when the school you wish to transfer to doesn't prefer those applicants. Just look to see whether the other universities you want to attend dissuade transfer students with a vocational background from applying. Remember, Cornell University accepted me after I acquired a degree in Paralegal Studies. Nonetheless, the mere fact that a school prefers that a candidate takes certain courses does not mean that a student who fails to complete those preferential course cannot attain admission. Schools are known to make exceptions by waiving academic requirements on a case-by-case basis. The University of California at Berkeley waived Foreign Language and English Composition requirements so I could gain admission. Applicants should never get discouraged.

Do not let this information dissuade you, however, from initially attending a four-year college, especially if you have the opportunity to enroll as a scholarship recipient. I know many transfer students who attended Ivy League universities after acquiring credits at a four-year institution. I have included some of these stories in this book. Make sure you make the most cost-effective decision when you are determining where to earn your credits, which you only seek to transfer to the four-year institution from which you hope to graduate. Why pay thousands of dollars at a four-year institution solely for course credit? In my personal opinion, it's just not worth it.

Chapter 7

Freshman Year – Fall Semester

So you've done it, right? You're a college student. But now you're wondering what steps you should take to secure your admission into the four-year school of your choice by tomorrow. Slow down. Take a deep breath. You still have a while to go. In this chapter, you will discover what steps you should take while you are in your first semester at your newly found educational institution. If you are currently beyond your first semester, take the information I give you in stride. Just use the information you find most applicable to your current situation and apply it where possible.

In the fall of 2003, I entered Manor College's Paralegal Studies program. I was a freshman. I remember walking around campus during my first day of classes attempting to immerse myself in my newfound surroundings. At the time, I didn't think about gaining admission into an "Elite" institution. I only knew that I wanted to perform well academically. I was no longer attending school using my parent's tax dollars, but rather the cash out of mine and my parents' bank accounts.

However, the financial cost wasn't my main incentive to perform well. I knew I wanted to go to law school. Deep down, I also wanted to show my friends and family that I wasn't the person who performed below par, time and time again. I wanted to demonstrate to everyone around me that I had the capacity to rise to the top and achieve academic success. During high school, there were times where I would push myself to perform well but I would soon revert back to my old ways after a few days. This time, when I tried, I knew I wasn't going to give up momentum. I had my goal. Little did I know that these thoughts were the revelations that would eventually drive me to attain admission into Cornell University.

Early on during my first semester, I made an appointment to meet with the Director of Student Activities to learn more about the student organizations on campus. By doing so, I acquired some insight into how Manor College's campus life worked. Somehow, I believed that if I became involved with Manor College's student activities, I would build my resume while meeting people who could provide me with invaluable experiences, which would aid me during the transfer application process. I assure you, that doing such, was the right decision.

I realized, however, that if I was going to achieve my goal of gaining admission into law school, my grades would have to mirror my aspirations. By excelling in college, I could foster relationships with professors who would eventually write recommendation letters on my behalf either for transfer admission or graduate school. As I eventually discovered, performing well academically was essential to obtaining admission into Cornell University as a transfer student. I realized that performing at my highest potential revealed my ability to thrive in a more challenging academic environment, which eventually led the Ivy League admissions counselors to disregard my high school transcript.

The Ivy League admissions counselors usually care about college performance the most during the transfer admissions process. For example, Yale University recognizes, as stated on the school's website, that, "As Yale is above all an academic institution, academic strength is our first consideration in evaluating any candidate. The single most important document in the application is the college transcript." Luckily, for this reason, my main focus during my first semester remained on my academics.

> "As Yale is above all an academic institution, academic strength is our first consideration in evaluating any candidate. The single most important document in the application is the college transcript."
>
> - Yale University Website

My courses during my first semester at my initial two-year college, Manor College, consisted of a general legal studies track. Although most students do not take such courses during their undergraduate education, I was on my way to earning an associate's degree in Paralegal Studies. I took Introduction to Law and Paralegalism, Legal Research, English Composition, Interpersonal Communication, Keyboarding, and Introduction to Computer Applications; these courses provided the building blocks for my career as a Paralegal. Nonetheless, becoming a Paralegal was not my goal. These courses were only a building block in my quest for academic success, which I hoped to use to catapult myself into a career as a lawyer.

When I enrolled in my first semester, I knew my college courses wouldn't be as easy as high school. But I didn't know which courses would cause me to struggle. I wasn't even sure if I could write well enough to achieve a grade higher than a "C" in my freshman English course. But, I gave it my all. The grades were second to my efforts to learn the information. And, of course, grading at my two-year college wasn't anonymous so I knew brown-nosing wasn't going to hurt. I mean, some kids might have disliked me for my blatantly obvious efforts to suck up, but they became envious of me anyway once I got into an Ivy League school. So, giving others a reason to dislike me early on wasn't really a bad thing.

It felt good to finally perform well academically. However, I have to give credit to the "Note Card Method." You may be asking yourself, "What is the Note Card Method?" It's a method that I have found ensures pure academic success while enrolled in an undergraduate education, which requires memorization and regurgitation. Prior to enrolling in Manor College, I had no idea how to internalize information. I realize others find it extremely difficult to learn information; however, I discovered it wasn't so bad once I figured out how to memorize efficiently.

The purpose of this book is not meant to teach you how to study; however, I will highlight what I believe is an invaluable method to learning information effectively; the method has been around for generations. Generally, most undergraduate examinations in college test rote memorization. Prior to enrolling in college, I didn't know how to store large quantities of information in my brain. Once I got to college, I used note cards to learn and retain such information. Now, I didn't put everything on note cards; though, I did make a lot of them. The information I wrote on the back was based on the information, which the professors highlighted during class. Because textbooks hold much more information than professors' review during class, I knew that my professors couldn't possibly test on everything. For this reason, I learned to cut corners.

I took my notes from class and put them on the back of note cards. After I memorized all of the information, I would just review my note cards repeatedly until the examination. This made exam time much easier. The method was also really practical because I could carry my note cards anywhere. I was well prepared by the time I had an examination because I would only memorize approximately twenty note cards per day and I would review the ones I made on previous days after I memorized the new note cards.

Sometimes you're not lucky enough to find an easy professor, so it is extremely valuable to make sure that you know how to learn efficiently. Also, once you get into the school of your choice, you will have to apply the same learning technique to the courses you take at your new institution.

This is why learning how "YOU" learn is extremely important. Take advantage of the Note Card Method and see if it works for you.

After learning how to memorize, I discovered that I could write a paper decently enough to keep up with the other students in my classes. However, I spent a lot of free time trying to figure out how to organize a paper so I could excel in my English course. The semester flew by much quicker than I expected because I spent so much time working on my school work. I found myself much more engaged than when I was in high school. Many of the headaches, however, that came along with high school carried over into my undergraduate education. Though, this time, I was much more prepared.

I remember coming home mid-semester with my progress report. My parents asked me how I was performing academically. Of course, I told them the same thing I told them during high school, which was that I achieved only A's and B's. They didn't believe me. You should've seen the look on their faces when I actually showed them my grades. That's right! All

A's, except for one "B." But, the semester was not over yet. I was determined to end my first semester with a flawless GPA. It was my chance to be perfect. I had a clean slate. With my parents off my case, I was able to focus my energy on performing well academically not because I was told to, but rather because I wanted to achieve that goal.

By the end of the semester, I was one assignment away from achieving a 4.0. I put all my energy into my work. The last paper I wrote for my English Composition course was draining. But I ended up accomplishing my goal for my first semester. My report card revealed 5 straight A's. I finally received a flawless GPA. What an accomplishment. No more C's or D's. I was satisfied, but the hunger for great grades and academic delight was just beginning. I didn't realize that achieving one objective would lead to an undying need to fulfill another goal. At that moment, my ego turned full speed ahead.

I remember questioning my parents about how I could use my college grades to my advantage. My parents weren't actually sure because neither my mother nor my father ever took part in the transfer admissions process. My parents told me to continue to perform my best and to apply to a few local schools but I already had my sights set on much bigger things. True, state schools would have been sufficient; however, I wanted to achieve what most people believed, for me at least, was unattainable. You got it. An Ivy League degree!

I wasn't quiet about my aspirations either. You should have seen everyone's reaction. Everyone was questioning how I could possibly get into an Ivy League school with one semester worth of good grades at a two-year college. Impossible? Wrong! Well sorta. One semester wasn't going to be enough, but at least I had my eyes set on a goal that unbeknownst to others was actually achievable. I recognized, however, that if I was going to gain admittance into an 'Elite' university I was going to have to prove to those colleges that I was able to compete with the best and the brightest. For this reason, I knew my grades would have to continue to come first.

First off, I would advise you that if you did not perform well academically while in high school or have failed to perform up to par during college, you should exert all your effort into performing well academically during the rest of your time at your current undergraduate institution. You need to recognize that performing well in college will negate your mishaps in high school. Although a flawless undergraduate GPA is not necessary, the higher your GPA, the better your odds are at getting into the school of your choice. I do, however, know a few people who did not achieve a 4.0 undergraduate GPA prior to transferring into an Ivy League institution.

During the transfer admissions process, admissions counselors make an individualized assessment of an applicant's application, which means the GPA is not the sole factor. But the stronger the GPA, the stronger the

> "Most transfer applicants present very strong college and university grades, but there is room in our review process to account for students whose grades may have improved as they changed majors or whose performance may have improved or changed over time."
>
> - Dartmouth College Website

application. If your GPA is not extremely high during your first semester,

69

don't fret. For example, the admissions counselors at Dartmouth believe, "Most transfer applicants present very strong college and university grades, but there is room in our review process to account for students whose grades may have improved as they changed majors or whose performance may have improved or changed over time." Statistics show that the first semester in college is commonly a lower GPA due to adjustment. So, just continue to work on your GPA.

As you work on your GPA, you must also attempt to foster relationships with your professors; these relationships will give you the ability to eventually obtain faculty recommendations, which is an essential part of the transfer application process. If you have yet to build such relationships, don't worry about it. You still have three semesters to go.

Getting great grades wasn't my only objective. During my first semester at Manor College, I became involved in every extra-curricular activity that interested me. Actually, if you honestly would like to know the truth, I became involved in any activity where I knew I could attain a leadership position. I actively participated in the organizations I joined because students do not generally acquire leadership positions during their first semester. I became involved in my campus' Legal Studies Student Association, Rotaract Club, as well as the Student Government Association. I had to lay the foundation so I would be first-up to run these organizations during my sophomore year. I also knew that if I kept up my GPA, I would have the opportunity to join the honors societies' on-campus, such as Phi Theta Kappa and Alpha Beta Gamma. Two-year college honor societies provide leadership and scholarship opportunities to members. So, by putting most of my energy into performing well during my first semester, I was also able to put myself in a position to acquire leadership opportunities later on in Manor College's honor societies. Remember, two-year colleges provide students with opportunities to participate in student activity groups on campus and most students don't take advantage of the resources. Thus, it is easier to acquire a leadership role at a two-year college than at a four-year school.

No matter what your grades are academically, you should join extra-curricular activities. Admissions counselors look highly upon transfer students who explore various extra-curricular opportunities because the Ivy League universities admit students who have a broad range of diverse experiences. Also, the more student groups you join, the easier it will be to acquire some type of leadership position prior to transferring. The position will give you something to talk about in your transfer applications. Leadership roles also convey to admissions committee members that you are a go-getter. The Ivy League wants to admit students who can potentially lead the country for future generations. So, even if you're offered a measly secretarial position, take it!

Extra-curricular activities can also help lessen the emphasis that a particular school places on your GPA. If your grades are just on par with the minimum GPA that a specific school considers competitive for an ordinary transfer applicant, you should become more involved in on-campus activities. Remember, the more you buff your resume, the better your chances are at gaining admission into the school of your choice.

Even though my first semester was just the beginning of my college education, I made every effort to attain great grades. By performing work at the collegiate level that surpassed my professors' expectations, my SAT scores became meaningless. The hard work also helped me build and foster relationships with professors, which eventually culminated into recommendation letters. Over time I realized that I would have to continue to preserve my fairly high GPA because I couldn't use my high school record to reveal to admissions counselors why they should let me into their school through the front door. And, by becoming involved in student activities on-campus early on, I had an easier time acquiring leadership roles, which looked great on my college transfer applications. Luckily, I could start anew even after sabotaging my high school record.

Chapter 8

Freshman Year - Spring Semester

Now, you're currently enrolled in your second semester, right?
Congratulations! At this point, you should have a better idea about
whether you can perform at a challenging academic level in college. If your
college academic record is currently outstanding, you should be excited. But
even if you have yet to perform well academically, you should know that there
is still time to work on your academic performance. Don't get discouraged.
Remember, academics are only one component to the transfer application.
As you continue reading, I will convey to you the key steps you must take
during your second semester at your initial undergraduate institution to
successfully transfer to the school of your choice.

During winter break, I opened up my course schedule for
the spring semester. I was so focused on my grades and my
curricular involvement during my first semester that I hastily
enrolled in a full course load without researching the professors
who taught the classes I was going to be taking. As I sat down
to look over my course schedule, I took out a notepad and

began jotting down the course names. I was scheduled to take Civil Procedure, Legal Writing, Fundamentals of Composition II, College Math, and Business Law. To the right of each course name, I wrote down the name of the professor who planned to teach each course. After completing this process, I then contacted other students who previously took these same professors. I questioned these students about each professor's teaching style. Where possible, I also used internet resources to research the professors to get a general idea about each professor's level of difficulty. For this, I primarily used www.ratemyprofessor.com. The website was, and is, an invaluable resource.

By researching the classes and the professors, I found out how much effort I needed to exert in each class to attain an "A." When I learned that certain professors taught the subject matter in a more concise and coherent manner, I chose to take that professor as opposed to another one who also taught the same course but was seemingly much harder. As you can see, I put a lot of effort into maintaining my existing GPA. I made sure to select both my classes and professors wisely because my grades mattered most in my attempt to transfer to an Ivy League university.

Before entering your second semester, you should make sure that you enroll in challenging classes because Ivy League schools do not look very highly upon "Mickey Mouse" courses. However, in order to make yourself a competitive applicant, you should make sure you do research to find out anything you can about the professors who teach the classes in which you are enrolled before the semester starts; this will ensure that you know what to expect. You can also make sure that you are taking the easiest professor if more than one professor teaches a particular course. Taking an easier professor doesn't necessarily mean that you won't have to learn the information; however, you will have a much easier time earning a high grade. Remember, the name of the game is to transfer. For now, you need to remind yourself that shortcuts do exist. I'm sure you know this; otherwise, you probably wouldn't be reading this book.

Although I found effective ways to increase my odds at getting A's, I also put my nose to the grindstone once again to hold onto the GPA I worked so hard to achieve my first semester. I continued to use note cards to commit information to memory. Most of my examinations were straight regurgitation. If I encountered an examination, which required me to apply information, then I would just use the information that I memorized to pick the best choice while answering the questions. During my second semester, I continued to perfect my primary study technique: The Note Card Method.

Although I knew that I had to put forth effort to ensure that I lived up to my own expectations while maintaining an immaculate GPA, I knew that I had to continue to actively participate in extra-curricular activities. As I've mentioned previously, I joined the Student Government Association as well as the Rotaract club. Despite the fact that I did not yet hold a leadership position in the Student Government Association, I was able to run for President of Rotaract. This position was not so hard to snag. I ran uncontested for the presidential position. I was also invited to join both the Alpha Beta Gamma and Phi Theta Kappa honor societies because I achieved a high GPA during my first semester. Just remember, however, that you don't need a 4.0 GPA to join. You only need to perform well enough to achieve the minimum required GPA for that particular honor society. I paid the small initiation fees to join because I thought the honor societies would look great on my transfer application. After joining, I was immediately elected Vice President of Phi Theta Kappa; these organizations provided me with additional opportunities to build my extra-curricular resume with leadership positions. I did not hold leadership roles prior to enrolling in college so these opportunities were beneficial.

I wasn't sure, however, whether just listing the leadership roles on my resume would be enough. For this reason, I made sure to actively participate in the groups in which I was involved. For example, I used my position as President of Rotaract to establish a talent show on-campus; the activity was a success. The organization used the proceeds from the talent show to fund a scholarship for incoming students. Of course, I participated. I lip sang to a pop group with the Vice President of the organization. The experience was memorable. The club was able to garner enough support from both commuter and resident students. What an opportunity! Although putting together the talent show was time consuming, it was a great idea. Making up innovative activities and community service projects for the student activity groups eventually helped during the application process; this is because the activities gave me something impressive to talk about during my applicant interviews and write about in my applicant essays.

You should focus on becoming heavily involved in your college's on-campus life especially if you have not done so already. If you joined extra-curricular activities during your first semester, you should find out whether the organizations elect leaders on a calendar year basis or academic year basis. If the organizations you joined elect new leaders on a calendar year basis, then the spots will open up in January, which is when you will want to take hold of those opportunities. This type of election allows you to hold the position up until your last semester prior to transfer admission; this means that you will not have to be actively involved your last semester. Also, if you have yet to enroll in any activities, then you need to get the ball rolling. You do not want to apply to Ivy League schools or any "Elite" institution for transfer admission without listing any extra-curricular organizations on your transfer application. Without even minimal participation in social organizations, your application will not reveal to the admissions counselors that you have what it takes to thrive in the Ivy League social environment. Moreover, participating in on-campus clubs opens up scholarship opportunities because certain outside organizations give scholarship money to students involved in certain extra-curricular activities. Also, your campus administrators cannot recommend you for transfer admission or scholarship opportunities if they do not know who you are and they will likely get to know you if you are highly involved in extra-curricular activities on your college's campus. You want to show the Ivy League admissions counselors that you are able to balance both your academics as well as your social life;

81

this is why extra-curricular activities are invaluable to your transfer application.

On an additional note, you might have already been accepted or are about to be accepted into an honor society on campus. When enrolled at a two-year college, your campus' honor societies usually invite students to join after completing one semester. If accepted into one, you should pay the meager initiation fee to join the organization. The honor societies will look phenomenal on your transfer application. You do not want to apply to the Ivy League universities or any other school without them. And, if you are accepted into more than one, take every society up on the offer if you can afford to do so. These organizations can provide you not only with leadership positions but also scholarship opportunities for transfer admission. Some schools have special scholarships, which are only awarded to honor society members. Do not lose out! This is especially true for your safety schools, which you should be applying to when you're filling out your transfer applications.

I recognized that working on my transfer resume, which included my GPA and extra-curricular activities, was half the battle. I needed to make a decision as to what schools I wanted to attend for transfer admission. However, this task was not too hard. All I did was print off a list of the top fifty schools on U.S. News & World Report. These schools were my target schools. Of course, I chose a few safety schools in which I would have happily enrolled had my plan not worked out the way I wanted. It gave me comfort to know that there were schools, which would easily give me scholarship money while accepting all my credits. For this reason, I looked into colleges who had dual admission or articulation agreements with my two-year college. But, my primary objective was to enroll in an Ivy League university. For these reasons, I researched all types of schools for transfer admission while compiling my prospective list of schools.

During your second semester, you should draft a list of schools where you desire to transfer. Because you need to ensure that you take classes, which are geared to the curriculum where you intend to transfer, it is preferable that you have an idea at this point where you would like to transfer. It is ok if you do not finalize this list until just before your sophomore year. Also, if you decide to add a school to your list during your sophomore year, the inability to take courses geared toward the school's curriculum will not necessarily impede your chances of admission as some schools waive admissions requirements for transfer applicants. But the more time you have to plan to take the recommended courses, the more competitive you will become during the transfer application process.

As you begin drafting your list, you should attend transfer fairs, which are offered at two-year colleges. You should also speak to transfer admissions counselors to find out what schools have dual admissions as well as articulation agreements with your current school. If you are enrolled at a four-year institution or you have the desire to transfer to a school that is not under a dual admissions or articulation agreement with your current school, you can utilize online and bookstore resources to research schools for transfer admission. Various websites are helpful including collegeprowler.com and usnews.com.

Although the process was a bit overwhelming, I realized that if I was going to transfer, I was not only going to have to draft my list of schools to where I wanted to transfer, but I was also going to have to find out where I could market myself as a transfer student. I knew, however, that I could not apply to every school in the nation because it would have been too time consuming. I not only researched schools but took the time to visit college campuses; this made the application process much more manageable. Although it was not necessary to visit schools during my second semester, I took the time to visit a few liberal arts colleges and national universities, which were close to home.

The first college I visited was Swarthmore during an open house. Although I was a bit intimidated, I had a pleasurable experience. I made sure to take a friend who was also looking into transferring schools because I knew it would make the experience less stressful and not as nerve racking. The downside to the open house, however, was that the information session was geared toward traditional students who wanted to matriculate directly from high school. For example, Swarthmore distributed literature on how many valedictorians they accepted from the number of high school graduates who applied. Who cares? I didn't. That rat race was one I didn't win and one I never cared to win in the first place.

The first Ivy League school I visited was The University of Pennsylvania. Of course, I wasn't able to follow along during the information session since most of the information was not applicable to me as the session was catered toward high school students. But, hey, at least I enjoyed the experience. I even bought a t-shirt. It felt great just to know that I was a prospective applicant. The moral of the story, however, is that most campuses fail to provide non-traditional applicants with any information regarding the transfer admissions process since most schools are more concerned with soliciting students to apply for admission as freshman. I realized that I would have to look elsewhere for information catered toward the transfer admissions process, which would include setting up appointments with admissions officers.

While you are in your second semester, I advise you to start researching the colleges where you would like to transfer. If you have an idea at this point where you want to attend, you should at least visit some college campuses to determine whether you actually want to apply. Once you compile a list of those schools to which you would like to transfer, take some time out on the weekends to visit the campuses that are close to home. If you currently don't have the time, you can visit these schools after you have a full year of coursework under your belt. You can also ask the admissions counselors at the universities where you intend to apply if there is anyone who is specifically knowledgeable about the transfer admissions process so you can learn more about the transfer admissions process for a particular school as the requirements are usually different.

If I started applying to schools without visiting college campuses, I probably would have ended up applying to too many schools; this would have cost way too much money in transfer application fees. But, don't let money discourage you from applying to the schools where you want to attain admission. Most schools will waive application fees for prospective applicants who cannot afford the high application fees. Because I could not afford an unlimited number of fees, I had to be more selective in the schools to which I applied. And, I didn't want to waste my time writing essays and taking course requirements to attain admission to every school in the country. Visiting these campuses will also save you time because you won't waste time filling out transfer applications to schools where you really can't envision yourself. Moreover, you must find out and fulfill the requirements for transfer admission for each school to which you apply; this is a time-consuming process.

Overall, my second semester provided me with the opportunity to focus on maintaining my existing GPA. Moreover, I spent more time becoming involved in on-campus extra-curricular activities. Acquiring leadership positions, joining honor societies, and establishing community service events became invaluable to my transfer application. Lastly, compiling a list of schools where I intended and hoped to transfer made the transfer application process much easier for me to navigate because I could focus on the transfer requirements for fewer schools.

Chapter 9
Summer in Limbo

So you've finally done it. You've finished your first year in college! Congratulations. At this point, you should either be waiting to receive your grades from last semester or you should have already received them. Either way, you at least have an idea about how you performed last semester. This should be an exciting time in your college career, especially if you have performed well academically. At this point, there are still many necessary steps you must take. Throughout this chapter, I will reveal to you the steps you must take during this critical time, which includes choosing where to apply as well as how to begin preparing your transfer applications. Even if you have not performed at a level that makes you competitive for acquiring admission into an Ivy League university as a transfer student, I advise you to apply. There are also many other colleges and universities to which you can apply where you might even be able to attend for free because of scholarship opportunities. Either way, following my method should save you nearly half the price on a four-year college education.

After I finished my freshman year, I could hardly believe what was happening to me. I was enthusiastic because I received straight A's for two semesters in a row. This astounded me. As I always performed below par in high school, I'm sure my grades astonished many other people as well. I told my parents that I only wanted to apply for transfer admission to prestigious universities since I performed well academically. Of course, they were a little critical. I mean who wouldn't be, right? My parents reassured me that I would more easily obtain admission to local schools in the area, but they encouraged me to take a few chances and apply to those schools where most students in the nation want to attain admission.

Don't let anyone discourage you from applying to your dream school. If I listened to those around me, I would never have acquired a degree from an Ivy League university. It was only by taking a chance and applying that I eventually ended up with the degree I received. I remember speaking to a college admissions counselor who specialized in transfer admission. She informed me not to apply to Cornell University as I did not have any shot of attaining admission. She directed me to apply to public state schools, which were sufficient but not desirable to me. This conversation might have well been my "Trigger Moment" for wanting to gain admission into an "Elite" school. I knew I wasn't going to have someone tell me what I could or could not do. For me, it was time to break barriers.

After my freshman year, I decided it was time to actually visit Cornell University. It was summer time, so I finally had the time to visit the campus without worrying about my academics. Before I arrived, I made sure to schedule an appointment to meet with the head of admissions. Based on my previous experiences, I felt as though the regular information sessions would fail to provide me with sufficient information regarding the transfer admissions process. Making the appointment was probably one of the best decisions I could have ever made.

As this was my first time meeting one-on-one with an Ivy League admissions counselor, I will tell you that I was nervous. The Ivy League environment can be extremely intimidating to an outsider. I knew, however, that my first impression mattered.

Although I didn't wear a suit, I wore a pair of slacks and a fine-pressed button-down, long sleeve shirt. I also went with my father, which made the trip much less nerve racking. The drive up seemed like it lasted forever even though it was only about a three and a half hour car ride to Ithaca, New York. When I reached Ithaca, it was not as warm as I had hoped, but of course, I didn't care. The mere fact of being on an Ivy League campus as a prospective applicant gave me feelings of warmth immediately. And because I was meeting with the head of admissions, I felt a sense of importance ricochet down my spine. I recognized, however, that I still had a long way to go until I secured admission. I had yet to officially apply to the school. I was only setting the foundation for my eventual acceptance into Cornell University.

Once I arrived at Cornell, I helped my father find a parking spot. Everyone on campus was friendly, and they were all willing to help us get to where we needed to go. Eventually, we arrived at the admissions office at Cornell University's School of

Industrial and Labor Relations. At the time, I had no idea that I would actually matriculate into the school. However, I continued to tell myself that I would get in no matter what, even though most other people probably thought otherwise. As far as everyone else was concerned, the odds were against me; or, so they thought. Little did they know that during the transfer admissions process, college admissions counselors literally "throw out" a transfer student's high school record and SAT or ACT score. The colleges have no use for the statistics because they are not factored into the U.S. News rankings.

The admissions counselor was extremely nice but I didn't show up just to show face. I wanted to ensure that I was taking the classes most suitable for transfer admission. I wanted to ensure that I was taking every class that I needed to take in order to secure my admission without hesitation. I knew that if I met the school's minimum threshold requirements, I would more easily obtain a spot on the roster because I would be a competitive transfer applicant. Overall, the meeting went extremely well.

During my trip, I received advice on what classes to take to stay on track for transfer admission. I also found out that I would eventually have to participate in an interview as part of the application process. I was, however, able to plant the seeds that I wanted to grow. The head of admissions knew who I was and knew that I was really interested in transferring to Cornell especially since I took the time to drive to the school just to visit without any readily apparent incentive. Enthusiasm and perseverance can work wonders for a student's admissions prospects.

During the summer preceding your sophomore year, you should make sure to visit the schools where you want to enroll while making it a point to set up a meeting with an admissions counselor. Because admissions counselors receive so many applications for transfer admission, it helps to make the counselors aware of exactly who you are because they are the ones who eventually make the ultimate decision as to who attends their institution. Putting a face to the application can actually make a difference. The more connections, the better off you'll be in the long run. Furthermore, visiting the campus shows admissions counselors that you are extremely interested in the school. Although I know transfer students who enrolled at Cornell without visiting the school prior to matriculation, visiting a school not only allows you to meet with admissions committee members but also ensures that you get a better feel for whether you will fit into the school's academic and social environments. You can only learn so much from a school's viewbook.

Because the summer following your freshman year is not as hectic as the school year, you should definitely spend this time visiting college campuses while researching the institutions where you want to transfer. It's ok if you cannot afford to visit every single campus. It's impossible to visit every school. You might be better off visiting a particular school once you get accepted. But I do advise you to visit the schools where you most want to transfer while making it a point to schedule a meeting with an admissions counselor. Doing so will reveal to the counselors at that institution that you're adamant on attending their school.

95

Not only did I spend the summer just before my sophomore year visiting colleges and universities, but I also took the time to research what requirements I needed to fulfill to make myself a competitive transfer applicant at each institution. After meeting with the head of admissions at Cornell University's School of Industrial and Labor Relations, I discovered that if I failed to fulfill certain requirements, I could never attain admission as a transfer student. Prior to the meeting, I had no idea that students were required to take certain courses to be considered for transfer admission. I also discovered what classes I needed to take to more easily transfer course credit. And, if I didn't take certain preferred classes, I would probably have been a less competitive applicant. For example, during the meeting, I learned that the admissions committee at Cornell University's School of Industrial and Labor Relations pretty much requires prospective transfer applicants to have completed Micro and Macro-Economics prior to matriculating. I, however, had to scramble to enroll as a visiting student at another college because I discovered this information out just before starting my sophomore year and my initial two-year college didn't offer those courses in the upcoming fall and spring semesters. Without those courses, I can likely say that I would not have attained admission into Cornell University.

From that point on, I sculpted my course schedule to ensure that I fulfilled the course requirements for every college where I intended to apply. I had no choice but to plan accordingly. I contacted each admissions office to find out the transfer admission course requirements for each school. I also went online to request information on course requirements for transfer students at each institution where I knew, or thought, I would apply. The time I spent organizing the information was well worth the payoff.

Prior to re-enrolling at your college for sophomore year, you should request informational packets from each institution where you know you are going to apply for transfer admission. Such packets should include the courses, which the school both requires and prefers transfer applicants to complete prior to matriculation. Remember, as a transfer applicant, you must specifically request information for the transfer process because your requirements will be different than those for students currently graduating high school. Even if you researched colleges while you were in high school, you must seek out information catered to the transfer admissions process. At this time, you need to ensure that you review all the course requirements for transfer admission. I have attached an appendix to the back of this book to aid you in maneuvering through the Ivy League admissions process. Thus, you will find requirements for transfer admission to each Ivy League institution in the back of this book. This way, you know up front what you need to do to secure admission without having to perform all the leg work yourself. You want to double check with the Ivy League institutions to make sure that you receive the most up-to-date information. Also, if you want information about other colleges or universities, please contact the admissions office at each school where you intend to apply.

You do not want to begin your sophomore year without enrolling in the courses that are required for transfer admission. Additionally, you want to ensure that you are enrolled in those courses, which your prospective schools *prefer in order to make yourself a more competitive applicant. As I've mentioned previously, the more courses you take that are preferential to the colleges and universities where you are going to apply, the more likely it is that you will attain admission into the school of your choice. Although you want to take as many of these courses as possible, you should also ensure that you finish the course requirements necessary to attain your associate's degree if you are enrolled at a two-year college.*

One goal, if you're enrolled at a two-year institution, is to secure your associate's degree prior to transferring to a four-year college. As some colleges are lenient with graduation requirements, you might be able to convince your current institution to waive a requirement or two to ensure that you are a more competitive applicant for transfer admission while still completing the necessary courses to attain your associate's degree. If you are currently enrolled at a four-year college, just focus on completing the course requirements for transfer admission to get the most credits while meeting the core requirements for your next school.

While speaking to admissions counselors, I not only spent time requesting information about the requirements for transfer admission, but I also requested the actual applications for transfer admission. Most schools, however, require prospective students to use the Universal Transfer Application. Some schools require prospective transfer applicants to fill out supplemental materials, which include additional essays for transfer admission. For this reason, I requested hard-copy applications to every school. I created a folder for each school where I stored every college application and additional correspondence that I received from each institution. I knew that if I failed to fulfill even one requirement while applying as a transfer student, the admissions counselors could have easily discarded my application without hesitation. Of course, I wasn't going to allow that to happen.

After or while you research each institution's transfer requirements, you must complete the most important task of all, which is the following: Request the college transfer application. This is the tool you need to gain admission into the school of your choice. Although these packets seem overwhelming since they are so extensive, you will feel a sense of accomplishment after you complete these applications during your sophomore year. You'll also discover which schools require you to use the Universal Electronic Application. You'll also discover whether certain schools have supplemental materials that you have to complete as well. However, you don't have to start filling out the applications right away if you are applying for fall admission of your junior year because the applications do not have to be submitted until early spring.

As you review the applications, you will realize that each school requires a certain number of essays for transfer admission. Some even require interviews for transfer admission. For each institution, write a list of the requirements that you must fulfill, including the number of faculty recommendations and applicant essays. Failure to complete one requirement may result in forfeiture of a possible opportunity of enrollment.

Prior to entering sophomore year, I compiled a list of colleges and universities where I intended to apply for transfer admission. I knew that failure to include a particular college in the list was not going to stop me from applying. Nonethless, compiling the list was vital. I needed to spend the remainder of my summer figuring out what requirements I needed to fulfill to secure admission to the college of my choice. I needed to figure out if I should enroll in more courses at another college as a visiting student to fulfill transfer requirements. Moreover, I continued to finish the courses required to attain my associate's degree while still ensuring that my transfer applications would be the most competitive they could be for transfer admission. I was determined to make the best use out of the time and money spent at my two-year college.

Chapter 10

Sophomore Year – Fall Semester

Wow! You're finally entering your sophomore year in college. What an accomplishment. You're half-way done at your initial undergraduate institution and one-fourth the way through the completion of your bachelor's degree. Currently, where you stand academically is a large factor in where you will acquire admission as a transfer student. As most Ivy League universities do not allow students to transfer after acquiring more than two years worth of college credit, you only have one more year to increase your odds at getting into the school of your choice. Nonetheless, not all hope is lost. If you are currently at a two-year college, you can utilize the resources available at your school while attaining admission to a college or university through a dual admissions or articulation agreement. You can also seek to apply to a particular school where your academic credentials are most competitive. During this semester, your focus should not only be on your academics and extra-curricular involvement, but on filling out your applications for transfer admission. As you continue to read, I will reveal to you what steps you should take as you get ready to dive right into working on your transfer applications, which includes writing your essays and obtaining faculty recommendations.

As I re-entered Manor College for another year, I realized things were different. I was no longer a freshman. However, it wasn't just that I was no longer a part of the incoming class, which made me realize things were much different. I knew that by attending Manor College as a sophomore, I was going to be treated like a senior; this was definitely an advantage with respect to extra-curricular activities.

Even though I achieved an immaculate GPA while actively participating in the extra-curricular organizations at Manor College during my freshman year, I knew that I could not allow myself to go under the radar just yet. There were other opportunities, which I had yet to seize. For example, I had not yet run for Student Government President. I thought this position could further help me secure admission into Cornell University and any other school for that matter. When I returned to Manor College that fall, I retained my current leadership positions while seeking out new ones to further buff my transfer resume. I was becoming a bit obsessive, but I didn't care. I knew what my goal was, and I knew that the more I accomplished, the easier it would be for me to acquire admission as a transfer student to one of my dream schools. I'm sure I could have applied to the same schools with fewer credentials with the same chances of admission but, at the time, I didn't want to run the risk.

As I've said previously, extra-curricular activities are an invaluable asset for any college transfer application. If you joined clubs or organizations during your first year, you need to check to see if those clubs or organizations are holding elections for new officers. If so, you need to make sure that you run for at least one election. If you have already secured a leadership role, you are in a good spot. Holding one leadership position is probably enough to convey to admissions counselors that you have the skills to survive in the Ivy League social community. Most students who initially enroll at a four-year college will generally not be able to secure leadership roles. So, if you can acquire a leadership position, you will put yourself above the rest of the pack during the transfer admissions process. Just capitalize on the foundations you built during your first year in the extra-curricular organizations you joined; this will make it easier to attain leadership positions during your second year. Who knows? You might end up running uncontested due to the lack of interest in your college's extra-curricular programs. You will have an advantage in obtaining one of these roles since there is generally less on-campus involvement because most two-year colleges are predominately commuter schools.

At some point, I became interested in acquiring a leadership position in Manor College's Student Government Association. Luckily, I was able to run uncontested for Student Government President. Moreover, the Student Life Administrator, with whom I met when I first enrolled at Manor College, selected me to serve as the Student Affairs Representative on the Board of Trustees.

When you first started reading this book, I emphasized the importance of learning the ropes at your newly found educational institution. The relationships you fostered early on may become vital to securing credentials, which will aid you during the transfer application process. Though, don't fret if you do not have the same credentials I acquired. Many students who are admitted into Ivy League institutions as transfer students have other qualities, which Ivy League transfer admissions committee members' desire. Participating in organizations outside your college campus will add value to your transfer application. If you participated in outside organizations, then you should highlight these activities in your transfer application to convey to admissions counselors that you are not only academically but socially skillful.

I spent the remainder of my first semester during sophomore year continuing to perform at my maximum potential; though I not only had to perform well academically at Manor, but I also had to perform well at the other institution where I was enrolled. As I mentioned previously, I needed to enroll in Micro and Macro-Economics to make myself a competitive transfer applicant at Cornell University's School of Industrial and Labor Relations. For this reason, I enrolled in Micro-Economics at Arcadia University in Glenside, Pennsylvania, in the fall of 2004.

I then enrolled in Macro-Economics at the same school in the spring of 2005. I received A's in both Economics courses. Luckily, I performed well enough at Arcadia to ensure that my overall combined GPA did not suffer. The schools where I applied for transfer admission required me to submit an undergraduate transcript from every school that I attended.

You need to ensure that if you enroll at an institution other than the one where you are enrolled full-time, that you perform well academically at both schools. The schools where you will apply will most likely request undergraduate transcripts from each institution you attend even as a visiting student. For this reason, you must ensure that you put your energy into performing well at every institution where you enroll prior to transferring. Moreover, you need to find out whether you even need to enroll at a different institution; this is why it is vital to know what course requirements you need to fulfill to secure your admission as a transfer student at the college of your choice. If your current institution does not offer a particular course, then you will need to enroll elsewhere to fulfill the requirement. You also want to make sure that the requirement is completed prior to completing your first two years at your initial undergraduate institution. If you were to take the course during the summer preceding transfer admission, you would not have the course on your college transcript when you apply.

As if grades and extra-curricular activities weren't enough, I learned that transfer admissions committee members wanted me to solicit faculty members to write recommendations on my behalf. Mentally exhausting, huh? Each transfer application required me to ask faculty members for letters of approval. In order to fulfill this requirement, I approached my Calculus professor, my English professor, and my Legal Writing professor. These were the professors with whom I fostered relationships, both inside and outside the classroom, during my first year at Manor College. Because I began fostering such relationships as soon as I enrolled at Manor, it was much easier to secure these letters for my transfer applications. Although I didn't realize the importance at the time, it was necessary to build those relationships to help me secure transfer admission to any institution. The professors were also more inclined to write letters describing me on a personal level. I made sure to ask these professors to write letters as early as possible. I didn't want them to get bombarded with other things, which would otherwise inhibit them from writing recommendation letters for me.

You've probably already requested applications for transfer admission to almost every school where you intend to apply; however, you need to find out which schools require faculty recommendations. A general rule to keep in mind is that most schools require these letters. You just need to find out how many letters each college or university wants you to submit in order to be considered for transfer admission. Both hard-copy and electronic applications will reveal this information. If the application fails to reveal the number of letters required, you can contact the admissions office to find out. Either way, you need to determine how many letters you need to secure admission to the school of your choice. Finding out early on provides you with ample opportunity to ask certain professors to write the recommendation letters that you need to help you secure admission. If a school requires you to submit a specific number of recommendations but allows for more, you can send more if you feel the need. However, you do not want to bombard the admissions committee members with too many letters. I, personally, sent three letters with every application unless instructed otherwise.

In determining who to ask for recommendations, you need to recognize that there are two different types of faculty recommendation letters; they are either academic or personal. First, you can secure a recommendation letter from a professor who knows about your academic work product. These letters convey to admissions counselors your work ethic in the classroom. If you can procure such a letter from a professor who holds a directorship in the institution where you are enrolled, you might be able to add a little bit of prestige to your application. Second, you can secure a recommendation letter from a professor who you not only had for a particular class, but who also knows you fairly well on a personal level. The latter of these two letters can add value to your application because the author can write something more personal about you.

Remember, it's not as hard as you might think to get a teacher to write you a recommendation letter. Who knows? They might even feel honored

you asked. Even if you feel as though a particular professor will not write
you a recommendation letter, ask the professor anyway. You have nothing
to lose. Although some professors may seem intimidating, you should not let
this stop you from inquiring. Most professors are willing to help students
secure admission to other colleges and universities even if it means taking
time out of their busy schedules to write a letter. I've never had a professor
refuse to write a letter on my behalf. I'm almost positive no professor would
turn down your inquiry either if you're a decent student.

Although I knew what course requirements I needed to
fulfill, I still needed to finish requesting the transfer applications
for each institution to find out what requirements other than the
faculty recommendations I needed to complete. After
requesting every application, I began sifting through the
requirements for transfer admission for every university, which
included the steps I needed to take; this included the essays I
needed to write. At the time, only some colleges and universities
used the Universal College Application for transfer students. As
of now, most colleges and universities use the system to

streamline the transfer application process while making it much easier for the admissions committee members to select the most competitive applicants. Nonetheless, I researched what schools required me to fill out supplemental forms, which accompanied the primary application. This process was exhausting, but I figured that if I continued to push forward I would have a shot at attaining admission into some prestigious schools. I also checked out what schools required interviews to ensure I met every requirement.

At this point in the process, you must find out whether the schools you're applying to require you to fill out the Universal College Application for transfer admission. You can visit the organization's website at www.universalcollegeapp.com. The website will provide you with the electronic application for particular colleges and universities as well as a link to look at supplemental application pages. Although you have until the spring semester to complete your college essays if you are applying for fall admission of your junior year, you want to get a jumpstart on figuring out how many essays you must write for each school. Your applicant essays will be much stronger if you have more time to critique them. If you start early, you can make sure your essays are grammatically and logically correct. Please don't forget: Edit, Edit, and Edit!

I spent a lot of time working on my college essays. I needed to convey to the admissions counselors at each school why I wanted to attend their institution. I also figured it would be beneficial to reveal why and how I transformed from the student I was in high school to the student I was in college. For this reason, I spent a lot of time writing, crafting, and editing my admissions essays. I figured these essays would be given a lot of weight during the transfer admissions process. I knew I could only reveal so much through my college application, which meant that my college essays were the most vital component in revealing my ability to write as well as convey my desire to attend a particular institution. The essay was my primary mechanism to attract an admissions counselor's attention. Now, I'm not going to teach you how to write an essay in this book; however, I will at least provide you with the unedited essay that

I used, which helped me gain admittance into Cornell University though the back door. The following blurb is one essay I wrote for my Cornell University application:

Creative Essay on a Reflective Quote

The answers to life's questions are always on a gradual course of progression, and yet with time and maturity, I have come to realize that the compass for my path has always been before my eyes. My life is reflective upon the quote, "Two roads diverged in a wood, and I – I took the one less traveled by, and that has made all the difference. This quote, which is taken from a poem written by Robert Frost, shows a growing portrayal and close resemblance to the course that I have taken during my lifetime. As I progressed through my high school education, I constantly questioned where I would see myself as I got older. I was never a follower and did not like to conform to the structures that society had laid out for me, so I would sit in class and ponder my thoughts, not fully realizing the opportunities that were right in front of my eyes. Over time, I began to realize that if I was going to get somewhere in life, I was going to need to learn the skills and academic tools necessary for my success, thereby taking an individualized path to lead me into the future. There was a moment during my senior year in high school when I decided I wanted to become an influential figure in society, but I knew that in order to do this, I would have to take advantage of every opportunity that would come in my direction.

My experiences throughout my secondary education coupled with my goals for the future, both strongly influenced my decision to strive for a high level of academic achievement. I have always had an interest in our government and the legal system, so I decided that a career in law would benefit me in every respect. I then came to realize that in order to get into an esteemed law school, my scholastic achievements would have to portray what I am actually capable of. This was when I began to seriously evaluate where I stood academically. My desire for learning new things had finally come; but at a time when I could benefit from this situation, harsh realities still proved that my high school record did not portray my academic abilities. I then integrated views from different perspectives and began to formulate goals that were original in stature. I began to feel a great personal satisfaction that came from the personal enrichment of my academic commitment. This allowed me to subconsciously take a route that was far different from many other students my age.

During high school, I was not actively involved in my studies, yet my passion for learning new things about different subject matters was just evolving. Like many individuals, my drive to learn came at a point relatively late in my education. I never had the insight to realize my own intellectual/academic capabilities. As I entered into post secondary education, my goals and ambitions began to fuel my academic studies. Through hard work and determination, I began to develop an understanding of a wide array of academic subjects, and started to excel in many new areas of study. As far as becoming intellectually intrigued by new knowledge and having greatly increased my involvement in my school's academic and social environment, I am far from being compared to many students. This is because many of my peers, who are academically involved in my college campus, are students who excelled in high school. My interest in learning has added to my depth of participation in classroom discussions, as my thoughts now begin to overflow with new ideas and concepts.

My increased love of learning and leadership roles in my school have led me to become more service oriented, and have given me the ability to benefit those who are less fortunate. By involving myself in these various service opportunities I have expanded my point of view about the world around me, and have enriched my life with many new relationships and diverse experiences. Through this path that I have taken, I have met many people that have been very influential in my life. These influential individuals have helped me to grow into a more mature student, which has also provided me with the ability to become an avid leader, akin to many high-profile leaders in today's society. By becoming a leader, I am able to construct my own ideas and take part in a social structure that I can best conform to.

I now look upon my high school education not as a detriment, but as a learning experience which helped push me in the right direction. The path that I have taken may be the reason for my commitment to education, which has also enabled me to aim for my goals and warrant to become a successful future leader. There are very few people who can take a position on their education and come to the realization that they have taken an unrighteous path. There are even less people who come from this type of educational background and ultimately make something out of themselves. With my new appreciation for learning, and the personal enrichment that I have acquired through community service and leadership roles, I believe that I have performed a one hundred and eighty degree transformation in the right direction. Along with the help of highly qualified scholars and professors, I am using the present and the future as a way to indulge my intellect and fill my mind with new material. I know that my determination has pushed me and will continue to direct me towards my path of originality, which will allow me to meet my career goals as I proceed with the utmost respect for higher education and my capacities as a learner.

Through my essay, I attempted to convey to the admissions committee members that I recognized the importance of education and how it affected the world as well as my future. I revealed to the committee, through my essay, that even though my high school academic record was not the greatest, I could recognize my own faults. And, I showed that I was willing to move forward with the utmost respect for higher education. I conveyed how my past academic performance shouldn't hinder my opportunities for the future.

If you're attempting to break in the back door to any college or university after performing either below par in high school or sub-par on the standardized admissions tests, you're better off admitting it in your transfer essays while informing the committee why you're a much better student and how you will now be an invaluable asset to their academic community. People are usually empathetic and generally like to help others. For this reason, they may feel as though they can make a difference in your life if you're up for the challenge, and they believe, based upon your initial college performance, that you can either meet or exceed their expectations for academic performance.

Essay topics, however, can vary depending upon the school; this information is usually set forth in the supplemental application to the universal application or in the hardback application that the school provides. Some applications inform you that you may include additional essays. But as I said previously, don't overdo it when a school permits you to add something extra to an application. Use the opportunity only as a chance to convey to committee members something that you believe will be influential on their decision to admit you as a transfer student. These supplemental forms or hardback applications may also include other documents, which you will need to fill out prior to the submission deadline. For example, some colleges require students to have professors fill out mid-term progress reports halfway through the final semester to reveal a student's current academic strengths and weaknesses. Remain mindful of all the requirements.

During my first semester, sophomore year, I spent time taking courses, which I knew appealed to admissions committee members at each institution. Furthermore, I learned how important building relationships with faculty members early on was after I began approaching professors to solicit faculty recommendations, which most schools required as part of the transfer application process. Moreover, I had more time to edit and critique my essays before I submitted them with my transfer applications because I started writing my essays during the fall semester. Finally, although the entire process was time consuming and exhausting, I knew the payoff would be huge if everything went according to plan.

Chapter 11
Sophomore Year – Spring Semester

Amazing! You are finally in your last semester at your initial undergraduate institution. If you've followed my advice from the very beginning, you should be about to graduate with an associate's degree from a two-year institution. Or, you should have at least accumulated enough credits at a cost-effective price at a four-year institution, which you will attempt to transfer to your next college or university. Either way, you should be in a good position to transfer to an Ivy League institution, or any other school, to attain your bachelor's degree for nearly half the price. Now you're probably realizing that time flies by when you're extremely busy. When you started college, however, you probably thought that the past year and a half would feel like forever. Hang in there! You're finally in the home stretch. This semester should be much easier as you have already compiled your applications. You've probably begun working on your essays for transfer admission. And you're not far from mailing out or electronically submitting your applications. There are only a few things left for you to do this semester to secure your admission to your next college. But, most of all you should live a little and have fun. You deserve it!

By the time I entered Manor College for my fourth and final semester, I was well acclimated to the college's academic and social environments. I wasn't attempting to learn the ropes anymore. I was pretty much showing others how to climb them. As I knew this was my last semester, I performed the same way I did the previous three semesters. After reviewing the college applications, I discovered that my grades during my last semester actually mattered. Transferring is not like getting accepted straight out of high school. Most seniors slack off because they realize their grades no longer matter. College admissions counselors, however, still scrutinize transfer students' academic performance during the final semester. This is evidenced by the fact that most prestigious colleges and universities require prospective applicants to fill out a mid-term progress report, which the students are then required to get their current professors to sign. Because most colleges do not give out grades until after the semester is completed, students must make sure that they inform each professor about the importance of the report. One professor thought I wasn't going to receive an "A" in the course as my final grade because I achieved a "B" on my mid-term examination; however, I assured the professor that I would strive to attain an "A" and that there was no doubt in my mind that I would receive such a grade. After speaking with the professor, she signed off that she expected me to receive an "A." And, I did receive an "A" at the end of the course. This is just another reason why sucking up to your professors can only help you in your quest for academic success.

It is important to recognize that the most prestigious institutions require students to ask professors to fill out mid-term progress reports as part of the transfer application process. The schools provide this report in the transfer application materials whether primary or supplementary. Because of this, you need to ensure from the beginning of the semester that you are performing well in your courses because mid-term grades will be taken into consideration when applying for transfer admission. You cannot slack off now even if you have performed well for three semesters. Unlike high school, you will have a lower number of credits prior to enrollment, which means that a low grade in one class can also be extremely detrimental to your overall GPA. The admissions committee members want to see either constant or improved performance. If you start performing worse academically, it might reveal to the admissions committee that you might not perform well once you are admitted to their institution. Nonetheless, if all else fails, suck up to your professors to make sure that they at least write down a favorable mid-term grade on your progress report even if you're not on track to receive one. It can't hurt.

During my last semester at Manor College, I no longer had to actively participate in most of my extra-curricular organizations because other students were elected as student leaders. Many of the organizations' leadership roles were filled on a calendar-year basis. Therefore, I had more time to make sure that the grades I achieved my last semester remained competitive. Additionally, I had more time to devote to my transfer applications, which helped ensure that I received that coveted admissions letter from an Ivy League school. As transfer admissions deadlines were looming, I spent my spare time reviewing and editing my transfer applications, which included critiquing my essays. I had to make sure that my applications were ready for submission before the March deadlines.

At this point, you should be finalizing and submitting your transfer applications. You should also be putting the finishing touches on your college essays. If you took my advice, you should have started your essays last semester; this means that you should only have to edit or critique them. Remember to Edit, Edit, and Edit! At this time, you should submit your applications to each school on your list including your "safety" schools. Remember, you do not want to put all your eggs in one basket. You need to make sure you attain admission to at least one four-year college or university to make sure you are on track to securing a bachelor's degree; this is why dual admissions and articulation agreements with two-year colleges are valuable. If you fail to attain admission into an Ivy League university, or the school of your choice, you should recognize that the path you have taken can provide you with the opportunity to secure a bachelor's degree at, or less than, nearly half the price than if you enrolled immediately after graduating high school. Unlike most other people your age, you should not be shackled with student loan debt and forced into "voluntary" servitude to pay off your student loans for the next twenty-five years.

After I sent out every application, I knew that I all I could do was wait. It was an anxiety-driven experience. I knew that I had no control over my fate. I didn't have a hand in deciding which students these institutions would select for transfer admission. I recognized that I probably wouldn't attain admission into every institution where I applied, but I hoped that a few select schools would see that I was an excellent candidate for transfer admission. I, at least, wanted to receive one of those highly-coveted acceptance letters from an Ivy League school.

But, I knew one thing: I gave it my all. I knew that even if I didn't get accepted into a prestigious university, I was about to receive my associate's degree. Furthermore, I had scholarship opportunities, which I would not have received if I didn't perform well during my time at Manor College. For this reason, I could have gone to a less notable institution than Cornell for essentially no cost. At the very least, I was on my way to securing a bachelor's degree at a more cost-effective price than if I enrolled as a freshman.

Chapter 12

Acceptance

This is the moment you've been waiting for! You've received a letter in the mail informing you whether you've attained admission to the school of your dreams. Open it. You might be pleasantly surprised.

I remember receiving my first letter in the mail from an Ivy League institution. It was a rejection. I was extremely upset. I worked so hard for two straight years thinking the path that I was taking would give me a golden ticket into an Ivy League university. But, I lost sight of the bigger picture. I forgot that I applied to more than one Ivy League school. Then, it happened. I received my first acceptance letter. The letter, however, was not from a college or university ranked in the top fifty of U.S. News & World Report. Nonetheless, it felt good to know that I was accepted into a local university's honors program. At that moment, I knew that reaching my goal of attending a four-year college while working toward attaining my law degree from an accredited law school was in progress. I was even offered scholarship money, which would have nearly covered the entire cost of my education. I realized that I could attend a four-year college for next to nothing. For this reason alone, I recognized that it was worth working hard during my tenure at my initial two-year college because I could minimize the costs of attaining my bachelor's degree from a four-year institution. I no longer feared that I wouldn't secure admission into a four-year college to earn my bachelor's degree since I attained admission into one of my safety schools. The letter gave me confidence. And, I still had to wait to hear back from the other colleges and universities where I applied.

If the first letter you receive is a rejection letter, please do not get discouraged. I received a few rejection letters. Of course, this is why I advise you to apply to safety schools during the transfer application process. Just wait until you receive all your letters from each educational institution where you apply before you jump to conclusions. You have worked too hard to get discouraged. Nonetheless, working hard during your first two years at your initial undergraduate institution will serve you well in attempting to find a job upon graduation when you graduate with an associate's degree or a bachelor's degree. Moreover, you will attain your bachelor's degree at a more cost-effective price, especially if you attend a safety school through a dual admissions or articulation agreement with scholarship money. Remember, your energy has not been wasted.

You should have the opportunity to attend a four-year school as a scholarship recipient thereby saving yourself money in the long run. You should also receive an associate's degree, which no one can ever take away from you, if you enrolled at a two-year college. Furthermore, this process will hopefully allow you to graduate with less debt than you would have graduated with if you enrolled in a four-year college immediately upon graduating high school.

Nonetheless, if you spent the last two years at a four-year college because the institution provided you with a partial or full tuition scholarship, you may decide you do not want to leave your current institution. You can utilize your GPA to catapult yourself into a position with a noteworthy company while beating out your fellow peers for such a position when

133

companies come on campus to interview for employment opportunities. Furthermore, you might be waiting to hear back from more schools where you quite possibly could have acquired admission. My fingers are crossed for you.

After I received at least one acceptance letter to a safety school, I felt much better about my acceptance prospects. I now patiently waited for other schools to contact me. Eventually, I received an acceptance letter from Tulane University. I was ecstatic. It made me realize that my hard work in college really did pay off. I was finally accepted into an institution where I knew I would not have gained admission immediately after graduating high school. The admissions committee at Tulane University also provided me with scholarship money. But, this was just the beginning.

In a few weeks, I received a phone call from an admissions committee member from The University of California at Berkeley. I was excited! However, the school requires transfer students to fulfill so many requirements before matriculating. I learned that I failed to fulfill two requirements, which students needed to have completed to acquire a spot as a transfer student; these requirements were the Foreign Language and English Composition requirements. I failed to fulfill the Foreign Language requirement because Berkeley requires prospective applicants to complete either three years of Spanish at the high school level or two years at the collegiate level. I completed neither and I received a "D" in my high school Spanish II course. Furthermore, I didn't have a second advanced English class, which satisfied the school's English Composition requirement. I knew that the only way I would be able to secure admission to the institution would be for the admissions committee to waive these two academic requirements in my favor. After speaking with the admission's advisor, however, I also learned that Berkeley only accepts forty out-of-state transfer students. At that moment, I gave up hope; however, I'll assure you that it was unwise and hasty. I received a letter in the mail about one week later, which informed me that the admissions committee waived the academic requirements in my favor. The letter informed me that I was accepted into Berkeley.

If you are missing certain courses that schools require for transfer admission, you will not necessarily be knocked out of the running for admission. Admissions committee members have been known to waive requirements for students who they believe will thrive in their academic environment. Please continue to wait for your letters before you get discouraged. The "Breaking in the Back Door" methodology is meant to ensure that you make yourself the most competitive applicant for attaining a degree from the college or university of your choice at the most cost effective price. If you followed my advice, you might still receive that highly coveted admissions letter to the school of your choice or extensive scholarship money from another institution where you chose to apply.

I was so proud of myself for achieving what most people thought was unattainable. I acquired admission to one of the most highly sought after universities in the country; i.e., The University of California at Berkeley. Eventually, however, the time came. The date when Cornell University posted its acceptance letters on the admissions website. That morning, I signed on to the university website to view my fate. I wasn't sure whether I would receive an acceptance letter or a rejection letter, but I was hopeful.

There it was! The acceptance letter: "Congratulations! You have been accepted to Cornell University!" Those were the words I was waiting for. What people told me was unattainable, I now knew was achievable. I couldn't wait to spread the news. Most people probably wouldn't have believed me but I had the proof. At that moment, I was tempted to purchase an entire wardrobe from the bookstore because I couldn't wait to wear the Cornell University attire. It felt like I just won the lottery.

Receiving an acceptance letter from an Ivy League university is truly an exciting experience. However, receiving an acceptance letter from your dream school, which was at one time out of your league, feels amazing. Once you receive the admissions letter from the school of your choice, you should feel a sense of accomplishment. Even if you did not receive the letter you wanted, you should still feel a sense of accomplishment because you now have opportunities that would not have been open to you had you not performed

your best when you immediately enrolled in college. You are now on your

way to securing a bachelor's degree at the most cost-effective price. And

moreover, the grades you have achieved will complement the extra-curricular

resume you have built, which will look awesome to prospective employers as

well as on graduate school applications after you secure a bachelor's degree.

Remember, high school is not the only stepping stone to a successful career.

When everyone else is paying back student loans, you can just laugh about it

because you won't likely have the same burden looming over your head for

the next twenty-five years.

Nonetheless, it was finally time to make a decision. I had to choose where I wanted to enroll. Turning down The University of California at Berkeley was one of the hardest decisions I ever had to make. It was definitely a subjective decision, as both Berkeley and Cornell University are excellent schools. For this reason, I made my father actually go online and submit the form, which informed the admissions committee at The University of California at Berkeley that I was not going to enroll. To this day, however, I still have my acceptance letter. Never in a million years did I think I would have been given the opportunity to attend any of these institutions; let alone acquire admission to more than one. My high school record and SAT score did not pose a problem since my two years in college negated all my educational mishaps from high school.

If you attain an acceptance letter from more than one institution, you are going to need to make a decision. You are going to have to choose where you want to enroll. You might have not prepared yourself for this decision, but you are only going to be able to choose one school where you want to attend. For this reason, you need to make sure you know which school is your number one choice; this is why visiting the schools is important. The impression these schools left on your psyche should aid you in making your decision.

During my time at Manor College, I was able turn myself around to prove to admissions committee members at "Elite" colleges and universities that I had what it takes to excel in a competitive academic environment. For this reason, I now had the opportunity to show the Ivy League schools that I could compete with some of the best and the brightest. I was on my way to securing a bachelor's degree from an Ivy League institution. As I've said previously, I never thought my high school education would do anything for me. And, I assure you, I was right. Don't let others trample your dreams by telling you otherwise. Just follow my helpful tips on breaking in the back door to any college or university and you might just prove them, and yourself, wrong.

Chapter 13
Adjustment

Although this book is meant to teach you the tricks for attaining admission into the nation's most sought after colleges and universities, I feel compelled to reveal to you how I adjusted to the Ivy League academic environment. I'm sure not everyone's experience is the same; however, I can at least attempt to provide you with some insight on which obstacles you are likely to encounter. No matter what, you are not alone. Sometimes adjusting to the environment at your newly found educational institution is harder than breaking in the back door.

And there it was, my first day on campus as a transfer student at Cornell University. When I arrived at Cornell's campus, it was about 9:00 am. I did not sleep the night before. The drive was exhausting since I was going through sleep deprivation because the anxiety of living on my own for the first time was keeping me awake. I was finally on my own. To me, it felt like I was living in a whole new world. As soon as I arrived,

I was ready to move into my college's dorm on west campus. My dorm was called "The Transfer Center." We actually called my floor the fourth floor of the TC. I was lucky because I enrolled at an institution, which grouped all the transfer students together as if they were enrolling as freshmen. For this reason, it was probably much easier for me to become acclimated to my surroundings. Everyone who I lived with was new to the college.

After unpacking for about an hour, I finally met my roommate. He seemed really interesting. After a brief discussion, I learned that he was on the cross country track team at Cornell. And, of course, he was a transfer student who transferred from a four-year liberal arts college in Maine. As the day dragged on, I continued to meet more and more transfer students. I spent time getting well adjusted to my newfound surroundings as I began to explore the campus on my own. From this experience, I assure you that moving into the dorms on Cornell's campus was probably one of the best decisions of my life.

When you arrive at the college or university where you decided to transfer, you will find yourself surrounded by students who are either new or already acclimated to your college's academic and social environments. Living in a dorm is a great way to meet these people. If you don't live in the dorm, it will be harder to meet people unless you formulate study groups with students in your classes.

If your college offers you the opportunity to live in a dorm with transfer students, take the school up on the offer. You have nothing to lose and everything to gain. You will get to experience your new school with people who are in the same position. Who knows? You might even foster bonds that will last you a lifetime. If, however, you do not have the opportunity to room with other transfer students, living on campus will still provide you with resources, which will become invaluable to you during your time at your new school. You will meet people who can show you around campus and give you the ins and outs of campus life. I advise you to try out the dorms during your first year at your new school.

Orientation lasted about a week, so I used my time wisely to prepare for the upcoming semester. I took a few trips to the college bookstore; it was time to purchase my books for the semester. I was shocked because the number of books I was required to purchase for each class was more than triple the number of books I was required to purchase for any class I've ever taken before. At that moment, I recognized that it would take some skillful time management skills on my behalf to juggle the course load I was about to take on.

I wish I would have known sooner that my textbooks were going to cost me so much money because I would have made sure that I purchased my textbooks on Amazon or half.com. I could have saved myself some money. I will tell you that as I left the bookstore, I made sure to purchase some of the latest merchandise that Cornell University had to offer.

Make sure that when your semester is about to begin, you purchase your textbooks early. You may be able to purchase your textbooks online for an extremely low price. And, if you are willing to purchase used books, you can get them really, really cheap. You can easily check online search engines for used textbooks. You may realize that the number of books you purchase is much greater than the number of books you purchased while enrolled at your former institution. If you are required to purchase more books than you are used to, don't get overwhelmed. Remember, most professors cannot possibly cover the amount of work assigned during a fifteen week course. Just wait until your classes start. At that point, you can find out which information is really important and which information is not going to be tested. But, no one ever said that attending a prestigious university was going to be easy either. Remember, you're most likely only going to be spending two years at the school rather than four years because you obtained admission as a transfer student. That's what I like to call a lucky break.

Because orientation lasted one whole week, I was able to enjoy my time before classes started. I visited the fraternities. I went out drinking with fellow classmates. It felt like I was at overnight camp. But, I knew that it would most likely come to an end when classes started because I would have to make my academics my top priority. I still had my goal of attaining admission into law school. After I became acclimated to my new school, I realized that I would have to dive right into my academics. My classes were not easy. I struggled to perform the way I performed so many countless times before. I remember the first grade I received at Cornell University; it was a "C." Of course, this really meant nothing to anyone else, but it meant something to me.

I felt like a failure. I was used to perfection. I remember people telling me that I would probably be unable to perform at the same level that I performed at while I was enrolled at Manor College. I refused to believe them until I received my first grade. I remember calling my father as heavy tears rolled down my cheeks. I told him that I wanted to come home and no longer wanted to attend Cornell University. He told me that was acting crazy. I knew that the pressure I put on myself at Manor College was the same that I was putting on myself at a more rigorous institution. However, after some reassurance from my family, I knew I couldn't give up. I worked so hard to ensure that my grade in that class would not suffer for the "C" I received on the exam. I really wasn't used to the bell curve system. I didn't realize that the "C" was actually an "A." I never thought for a second that I would have ended up with an "A+" in the class; however, this is what happened at the end of the semester.

You should recognize that the classes that you enroll in at your new institution might be much harder than the classes you took while enrolled at the two-year or four-year institution where you were enrolled prior to transferring. For this reason, you need to prepare to work just as hard if not harder. Just remember, however, that the time you spend at your new school is not going to be for the rest of your life. You will most likely only be enrolled at your new institution for two years but these next two years will have an impact on where you end up professionally as well as academically. If the school admitted you, then you should recognize that you deserve to be there. The admissions committee members believed in you. Now, you must believe in yourself. You can perform just as well, if not better, than your peers. Also, most institutions like Cornell University curve the grades at the end of the semester, so you might end up performing much better academically than you may have expected.

When I enrolled at my new institution I needed to take the steps necessary to feel secure in my new academic environment. For instance, I found living conditions that were better suited for becoming acclimated to my new campus. I also learned that course requirements were much more demanding at Cornell; this is why I will inform you that you need to work just as hard, if not harder, than when you were enrolled at your initial undergraduate institution. I had to utilize the same study techniques that I mastered during my time at Manor College and apply them while I was in attendance at Cornell University. I attained admission into Cornell, which meant that the admissions counselors had confidence that I could succeed.

In conclusion, I'll leave you with the motto I began to live by when I started studying at Cornell: "Work hard, play hard." But, most of all you need to remember to smile and keep your chin up. No matter where you're enrolled as a transfer student, if you successfully followed my advice, you broke in the back door to an institution, which you probably couldn't have acquired admission to immediately upon graduating high school. Furthermore, you're most likely paying less than half the price for a college education, which is something you might not have been able to do if you enrolled in a four-year college immediately after graduating high school. And, this is all because you put your nose to the grindstone and worked hard during your first two years in college. What did you have to lose? Not a thing.

Chapter 14

Interviews with Ivy League Transfer Students

Anthony Scandariato, Cornell 14'
(Community College Transfer)

Anthony transferred to Cornell University in August of 2012 from County College of Morris, which is a public community college in New Jersey. Anthony has a story comparable to some other high school students who never had their sights set on attending a prestigious institution. Anthony claims that he achieved a 3.1 GPA in high school. In fact, he failed all of middle school so he was sent to a remedial high school specializing in teens with behavioral and academic issues. After two years, however, he returned to his district high school where he struggled. Anthony informed me, "I chose County College upon graduation to hit a reset button on my life. I was elected Student Government President, co-founded a club and did everything I could to get involved and be the best person I could be."

As for Anthony's thoughts on attending an Ivy League institution, Anthony didn't think he would attain admission into Cornell, but he really liked being around intelligent and motivated people. Anthony graduated from County College of Morris with a 3.96 GPA and an Associate's degree in Business Administration. He graduated Summa Cum Laude. Anthony's advice for other students looking to break in the back door to the Ivy League is, "Never dwell on your past – you could always turn it around and change your life for the better. And, do not ever give up!"

Aleksey Dmitrenko, Cornell 07'
(Community College Transfer)

Aleksey transferred from Northern Virginia Community College to Cornell University. It took Aleksey three years to complete a two-year program while working full time. Aleksey started out at his community college only taking two classes per semester during his first year but thereafter he became much more aggressive in his course selection. Aleksey claims that the hardest thing to adjust to in the Ivy League community was the amount of work. Aleksey states, "The amount of work was definitely a lot more at Cornell than at Northern Virginia Community College. Northern Virginia Community College prioritized for you what you needed to know, which made it easy to get the work done and helped with retaining information. Cornell, however, added a lot more color to each topic. It was more real so you had to learn how to prioritize and become much more efficient."

Aleksey made the decision to attend Cornell; however, he was looking at a lot of great institutions most of which were not in the Ivy League. Aleksey chose Cornell because, "... the opportunities offered to [him] at Cornell along with the financial assistance were unmatched by any other school." Furthermore, Aleksey claims that, "... the thing he valued the most about transferring to an Ivy League school were that other students were striving to get somewhere in life, which elevated his game."

Additionally, "... the small student to professor ratio enhances learning, and the recruiting opportunities are amazing because you can interview with all the top companies." While enrolled at Northern Virginia Community College, Aleksey achieved a 3.9+ GPA.

Aleksey advises potential transfer candidates to, "... spread out both fun and difficult courses over the entire time spent at the initial college while ensuring that a solid GPA is maintained." Furthermore, "... if there is a particularly tough course you want to take, you could consider taking it in your final semester to keep your GPA higher during the application period. However, you do need to show your future school that you can get the work done." Moreover, Aleksey's advice to each prospective transfer applicant is to, "... identify a few schools that you are interested in." He says that you should, "... visit two or three schools and talk to the Dean of Admissions. Talk to the students about what they like. The experience should create a bond between you and the school and make you work harder to attain admission." He further states, "You should be excited about being able to choose where you want to go."

Aleksey's advice doesn't stop there. He also believes that, "... you should speak to your professors about where you want to go. You will need recommendations from them anyway. But, your dialogue with your professors should start early on. When you eventually ask for a recommendation, don't just ask for a recommendation, ask for a great recommendation. Earn the recommendation." Also, "... identify other people that are looking to transfer because you could discuss the application process with them and review each other's applications." If Aleksey could leave you with a few final words about the transfer process, he would tell you, "Learning happens all around you, so don't forget to learn while you are on your quest to transfer. Good luck."

Chip Godfrey – Cornell, 08'

(Four-Year College Transfer)

Chip transferred from Colgate University immediately after he completed his freshman year. Chip claims that the hardest adjustment was meeting new people and starting at a new college all over again since he just went through the same process in the preceding year when he initially enrolled at Colgate. Chip chose to go to an Ivy League school because Cornell was the school at which he was accepted, with the largest student body and an enclosed private campus; however, he was not only invited to enroll at Cornell but also Penn, Amherst and Georgetown. Chip's GPA at his previous school was a 3.8. Chip's advice to prospective transfer applicants is to, "Make sure in your essay that you have a compelling reason about why you want to go to THAT school specifically. Also, explain what makes you different from other students they have considered for acceptance." Chip graduated from Cornell University in 2008.

Isaac Park, Yale, 13'
(Four-Year College Transfer)

Isaac transferred to Yale University after spending two years at Georgia Tech as a Chemical Engineering major. He transferred to Yale as an Economics major. Isaac believes that the Ivy League environment at Yale is much more demanding, which is ultimately satisfying to him. Isaac claims, "I'm much happier at Yale - much more integrated into the community - and so I have a lot more to do but much less time with which to do it. Basically, now I get four hours of sleep a night, and I wouldn't have it any other way." Moreover, he claims, "The thing I was actually worried about before transferring - increased academic rigor - turned out not to be a problem. Yale isn't much harder than Georgia Tech, just different (in all the best ways)."

Isaac is also a firm believer that he didn't choose the Ivy League. He states, "I didn't choose the Ivy League, the Ivy League chose me!" Isaac also claims that, "... it comes down to chance and/or luck at the end of the process." As Isaac phrases it, "There is only so much you can do; in the end, I just got lucky." From his own recollection, Yale accepted 29 transfer students out of 1070 applicants for his year; however, he doesn't believe his application was objectively better than any of the next 29 applicants that didn't get accepted. Isaac also claims that, "Yalies are happier, kinder, more energetic, more open-minded, and more liberal – in every sense of the word – than students anywhere else. (Can I actually know that? No. But I'm gonna say it anyway.) Being a Yalie is ultimately a statement of identity, and it's a label that I'm proud to wear."

Isacc took 73 hours at Georgia Tech over four semesters and achieved a 4.0 GPA. As for his advice to prospective transfer applicants, Isaac states, "Don't let transferring eat up a year of your life. Of course, keep your GPA as high as possible – but do what you really love, learn as much as you can, go to lots of parties, make tons of new friends, and, in your spare time, reflect on what you want. When it comes to writing a compelling personal statement, you'll want to be, above all, interesting, and being interesting takes a lot of self-awareness."

Nick Farruggia, Dartmouth, 12'
(Four-Year College Transfer)

Nick decided to transfer to Dartmouth College from the University of Pittsburgh as a sophomore. Nick claims that it was hard to adjust initially because, "... the social scene at Dartmouth isn't exactly compatible with the status of a transfer student. Greek houses make up essentially 90% of social spaces on campus – more than 65% of students rush, but not until the first term of the sophomore year." Moreover, Nick claims that he, "... unfortunately arrived on campus as a first-term sophomore, without the requisite year of vetting." Nick informed me, however, that he eventually recovered.

Nick decided to attend an Ivy League university because he wanted to be farther away from home. Moreover, he wanted to add some prestige to his resume with such an institution. Nick's

GPA at the University of Pittsburgh was a 3.95. Nick believes that the most vital part of a transfer applicant's application is the essay. For this reason, Nick thinks that prospective transfer candidates should, "... spend all of their free time making that application essay as tight as possible — you'll be one of maybe thousands of other kids your age with pristine freshman (and possibly sophomore) records."

ACKNOWLEDGEMENTS

My sincere gratitude and appreciation to Anthony, Aleksey, Chip, Isaac & Nick for their time in conveying their personal stories, which help convey the rigors of the Ivy League transfer admissions process. I would also like to thank Michael Zorn for his photographic contribution, my Dad for his time and creativity in creating the cover layout and design, as well as Sue Costantini for formatting the manuscript for publication.

Cover Design and Layout:
Frank S. Burstein

Formatting Manuscript for Publication:
Sue Costantini

Permission to Use Cover Panoramic Photo and Acceptance Letter:
Cornell University - University Photography

Headshot Photo:
Michael Zorn - Zorn Photography - www.mzorn.com

Permission to Publish Interviews with Ivy League Transfer Students:
Anthony Scandariato - Cornell, 14'
Aleksey Dmitrenko - Cornell, 07'
Chip Godfrey - Cornell, 08'
Isaac Park - Yale, 13'
Nick Farruggia - Dartmouth, 12'

APPENDIX:

VAULT

REQUIREMENTS TO IVY LEAGUE UNIVERSITIES

1) <u>Brown University</u>

2) <u>Columbia University</u>

3) <u>Cornell University</u>

4) <u>Dartmouth College</u>

5) <u>Harvard University</u>

6) <u>Princeton University</u>

7) <u>University of Pennsylvania</u>

8) <u>Yale University</u>

*The following information comes from admission websites for each Ivy League college and university. I have compiled such information for your convenience.

Brown University

Contact:

transferapp@ brown.edu

Tel: (401) 863-2378

Fax: (401) 863-9300

Address:

Undergraduate Admissions

Box 1876

45 Prospect Street

Providence, RI 02912

Application Fee: $75 or fee waiver

Application Packet: Common Application

Supplemental Packet: Required

Mid-Term Report: Allowed but not required

College Transcripts: Required

High School Transcripts: Required

SAT/ACT: Not required but preferred if taken

        Preferred: 1) SAT + 2 SAT II tests or 2) ACT

AP, IB, or A Level Exams: Not required but preferred if taken

College(s):
Brown College

Brown University

Address:
Office of Undergraduate Admissions
Box 1876, 45 Prospect Street, Providence, RI 02912

Contact:
Admissions Director
James Miller

Phone:
(401) 863-7940

Tuition:
$42,808 (2012-2013)

Interview Required:
No [Not available]

Enrollment:
Fall, Spring

Admission Deadline:
March 1st – Fall or Spring

SAT/ACT Required:
Preferred, not required

Competitive GPA:
Not Reported

Requirements:
At least 1 year collegiate study

Transfer Exclusions:
1. Liberal Medical Education Undergraduate Program
2. Brown – RISD Dual Degree Program

Course Credit: Courses are evaluated individually

Preferred Coursework: None

Required Coursework: None

Columbia University

Contact:

ugrad-ask@ columbia.edu

Tel: (212) 854-2522

Fax: (212) 854-3393

Address:

Undergraduate Admissions

 212 Hamilton Hall

Mail Code 2807

1130 Amsterdam Avenue

New York, NY 10027

Application Fee: $80 or fee waiver

Application Packet: Common Application

Supplemental Packet: Required

Mid-Term Report: Required

College Transcripts: Required

High School Transcripts: Required

SAT/ACT: Required

       Required: SAT II [Required, if taken]

AP, IB, or A Level Exams: Not required [unless already taken]

    - Credit is limited to 16 points for AP or IB exams.

College(s):
Columbia College
Columbia University, College of General Studies

Columbia University

Address:
Columbia University in the City of New York
Office of Undergraduate Admissions
212 Hamilton Hall, Mail Code 2807
1130 Amsterdam Avenue, New York, NY 10027

Contact:
Admissions Counselor

Phone:
(212) 854-2522

Tuition:
$45,028 (2012-2013)

Interview Required:
No [Not offered]

Enrollment:
Fall Only

Admission Deadline:
March 1st

SAT/ACT Required:
Yes
SAT II (must provide, if taken)

Competitive GPA:
3.5 GPA

Requirements:
At least 1 year of collegiate study

Preferred Coursework:
Not Reported

Required Coursework:
Not Reported

Cornell University

Contact:

admissions@ cornell.edu

Tel: (607) 255-5241

Fax: (607) 254-5175

Address:

Cornell University

410 Thurston Ave

Ithaca, NY 14850

Application Fee: $75 or fee waiver

Application Packet: Common Application

Supplemental Packet: Required

Mid-Term Report: Required

College Transcripts: Required

High School Transcripts: Required

SAT/ACT: Not required [unless already taken]

AP, IB, or A Level Exams: Not required [unless already taken]

College(s):
School of Industrial & Labor Relations
School of Hotel Administration
School of Human Ecology
School of Engineering
School of Arts & Sciences
School of Architecture, Art, & Planning
School of Agriculture & Life Sciences

Cornell University:
School of Industrial & Labor Relations

Contact:
Transfer Admissions Counselor
Ian Schachner

Phone:
(607) 255-2222

Tuition:
NY Resident: $27,045 (2012-13)
Non-Resident: $43,185 (2012-13)

Enrollment:
Fall, Spring

Address:
ILR School, 309 Ives Hall
Cornell University
Ithaca, NY 14853

Interview Required:
Yes [Phone Optional]

SAT Required:
Not Required

Admission Deadline:
March 1st – Fall
Oct. 1st – Spring

Required Coursework:
Two Courses – Freshman English (Composition) (6 Credits)
- AP (language & composition or literature & composition)
- Score of 4 or 5 is substitute for one course requirement

Microeconomics (or AP with score 4/5)
Macroeconomics (or AP with score 4/5)
College Algebra (or high school calculus/pre-calculus)
Three Liberal Arts Courses to fulfill distribution requirements:
- Science & Technology; Cultural Perspectives; Western Intellectual Tradition

Preferred Coursework:
AP Scores can be substituted for liberal arts requirements:
Science & Technology – Biology (or AP with score 4/5),
Environmental Science (or AP with score 4/5), Chemistry (or AP

with score 5), Physics B (or AP with score 4/5) Physics C- electrical (or AP with score 5), Physics C-mechanical (or AP with score 4/5)
<u>Western Intellectual Tradition</u> – European History (or AP with score 4/5) or U.S. History (or AP with score 4/5)
<u>Cultural Perspectives</u> - Comparative Government and Politics (or AP with score 4/5)

Competitive Applicants:
Minimum B+ GPA [3.3] and 24-30 credits

Additional Requirements:
Completion of 12 Credits Prior to Application

Cornell University: School of Hotel Administration

Contact:
Associate Director of Admissions
Heather Fortenberry

Phone:
(607) 255-6376

Tuition:
NY Resident: $43,185 (2012-13)
Non-Resident: $43,185 (2012-13)

Enrollment:
Fall, Spring

Address:
Hotel School, 180 Statler Hall
Cornell University
Ithaca, NY 14853

Interview Required:
Yes [Off-Campus Optional]

SAT Required:
Not Required

Admission Deadline:
March 1st – Fall
Oct. 1st – Spring

Preferred Coursework:
Chemistry [Lab Component] – High School or College
Three Years of One Foreign Language – High School or College
Math or Quantitative Courses [Highly Recommended]
Introductory Business Courses [Economics, Writing, Accounting]
Hospitality Work Experience

Required Coursework:
Completion of 12 Credits Prior to Application

Competitive Applicants:
Minimum B GPA [3.0]

Cornell University:
School of Human Ecology

Contact:
Senior Associate Director
Paul Fisher

Phone:
(607) 255-5471

Tuition:
NY Resident: $27,045 (2012-13)
Non-Resident: $43,185 (2012-13)

Enrollment:
Fall, Spring

Address:
170 Martha Van Rensselaer Hall
Cornell University
Ithaca, NY 14850

Interview Required:
No [Not Offered]

SAT Required:
Not Required

Admission Deadline:
March 1st – Fall
Oct. 1st – Spring

Requirements:
Design Students: Portfolio and Design Index
- Apparel Design, Apparel and Textile Management, & Interior Design

Transfer applicants must complete high school biology, and chemistry or physics; otherwise, courses must be taken as an undergraduate

Apparel Design* [Strongly encouraged to apply sophomore year]
Required Coursework: Introductory biology, chemistry, or physics, with lab (6-8 credits); English Composition (6 credits); Pre-Calculus or Calculus (3 credits); Introductory Psychology, Sociology, or Anthropology (3 credits); Portfolio and Design Index
Preferred Coursework: Statistics (3 credits); Introductory Macro-Economics (3 credits); Introductory Micro-Economics (3 credits)

Fashion Design Management

Required Coursework: Introductory Biology, Chemistry, or Physics, with lab (6-8 credits); English Composition (6 credits); Calculus (3-4 credits); Introductory Psychology, Sociology, or Government (3 credits); Introductory Macro-Economics or Micro-Economics (3 credits); Portfolio and Design Index

Preferred Coursework: Statistics (3 credits); History of Art (3 credits); Additional social science (Introductory Macro or Micro-Economics (3 credits)

Fiber Science

Required Coursework: General Chemistry with lab (6-8 credits); Physics with lab (3-8); English Composition (3 credits); Calculus (3 credits); Introductory Psychology (3 credits)

Preferred Coursework: Organic Chemistry with lab (6-8 credits); Statistics (3 credits); Introductory Micro-Economics (3 credits); Computer Science (3 credits)

Human Development

Required Coursework: Introductory Biology with lab (3-4 credits); Introductory Biology, Chemistry, or Physics, with lab (3-4 credits); English Composition (6 credits); Pre-calculus or Calculus (3 credits); Introductory Psychology (3 credits)

Preferred Coursework: Child Development (3 credits); Adolescent Development (3 credits); Introductory Sociology or Introductory Anthropology (3 credits)

Human Factors/Ergonomics and Facility Planning & Management

Required Coursework: Introductory Biology, Chemistry, or Physics, with lab (6-8 credits); English Composition (6 credits); Pre-Calculus or Calculus (3-4 credits); Introductory Psychology (3 credits); Introductory Macro or Micro-Economics (3 credits)

Preferred Coursework: Statistics (3 credits); Introductory Macro or Micro-Economics (3 credits); Introductory Sociology or

173

Anthropology (3 credits); Studio in two *or* three dimensional design
(3 credits)

Interior Design* [Strongly encouraged to apply sophomore year]
Required Coursework: Introductory Biology, Chemistry, or Physics,
with lab (6-8 credits); English Composition (6 credits); Pre-Calculus
or Calculus (3 credits); Introductory Psychology, Sociology, or
Anthropology (3 credits); Portfolio and Design Index
Preferred Coursework: Statistics (3 credits); Introductory Macro or
Micro-Economics (3 credits); Drawing (3-4 credits); Studio in two *or*
three dimensional design (3 credits)

Nutritional Sciences and Human Biology, Health, & Society
Required Coursework: General Chemistry with lab *(must be taken first
year)* (8 credits); Introductory Biology with lab (8 credits); English
Composition (6 credits); Calculus (3 credits); Introductory Macro or
Micro-Economics, Psychology, Anthropology, or Sociology
(3 credits)
- *[If Junior Enrollment: Organic Chemistry with lab required [8 credits]]*
Preferred Coursework: Organic Chemistry with lab (8-10 credits);
Statistics (3 credits); Introductory Nutritional Sciences (3 credits);
Additional social science (Introductory Macro or Micro-Economics,
Psychology, Anthropology, or Sociology) (3 credits)

Policy Analysis & Management
Required Coursework: Introductory Biology, Chemistry, or Physics,
with lab (6-8 credits); English Composition (6 credits); Calculus
(3 credits); Introductory Micro-Economics (3 credits); Introductory
Psychology (3 credits)
Preferred Coursework: Statistics (3 credits); Introductory Sociology
(3 credits); United States Government (3 credits); Ethics (3 credits)

Competitive Applicants:
Minimum B+ GPA [3.3]

Cornell University: School of Engineering

Contact:
Transfer Admissions Counselor
Scott Campbell

Phone:
(607) 255-5008

Tuition:
NY Resident: $43,185 (2012-13)
Non-Resident: $43,185 (2012-13)

Enrollment:
Fall

Address:
Swanson Center
102 Hollister Hall
Ithaca, NY 14853

Interview Required:
No [Not offered]

SAT Required:
Not Required

Admission Deadline:
March 1st – Fall

Required Coursework:
In order to enroll as a sophomore in a specific major, you must complete courses equivalent to those listed under "Sophomore Standing." To enroll as a junior, you must complete courses equivalent to those listed under "Sophomore" and "Junior Standing."

Biological Engineering:
Sophomore Standing
Calculus for Engineers
Multivariable Calculus for Engineers
Intro to Computing using MATLAB (or Intro to Computer Programming)
Engineering General Chemistry I
Intro to Organic & Biological Chemistry
Physics I: Mechanics
2 First-Year Writing Seminars

Junior Standing
Differential Equations for Engineers
Linear Algebra for Engineers
Mechanics of Solids
Principles of Biological Engineering (or Engineering
Thermodynamics)
Physics II: Heat/Electromagnetism
Biological Sciences, Lectures
Biological Sciences, Laboratory
2 Liberal Studies Courses

Civil Engineering:
Sophomore Standing
Calculus for Engineers
Multivariable Calculus for Engineers
Intro to Computing using Java
Engineering General Chemistry I
Physics I: Mechanics
2 First-Year Writing Seminars

Junior Standing
Differential Equations for Engineers
Linear Algebra for Engineers
Mechanics of Solids
Physics II: Heat & Electromagnetism
Physics III: Optics, Waves, & Particles
2 Liberal Studies Courses

Chemical Engineering:
Sophomore Standing
Calculus for Engineers
Multivariable Calculus for Engineers
Intro to Computing using Java (or Intro to Computing using
MATLAB)
Engineering General Chemistry I
General Chemistry II

Physics I: Mechanics
2 First-Year Writing Seminars

Junior Standing
Differential Equations for Engineers
Linear Algebra for Engineers
Mass & Energy Balances
Intro to Physical Chemistry Laboratory
Honors Physical Chemistry I & II
Fluid Mechanics
Physics II: Heat/Electromagnetism
2 Liberal Studies Courses
Biology Elective

Computer Science:
Sophomore Standing
Calculus for Engineers
Multivariable Calculus for Engineers
Intro to Computing using Java
Engineering General Chemistry I
Physics I: Mechanics
Object-Oriented Programming & Data Structures
2 First-Year Writing Seminars

Junior Standing
Linear Algebra for Engineers
Discrete Structures
Data Structures & Functional Programming
General Chemistry II
Physics II: Heat/Electromagnetism
2 Liberal Studies Courses

Electrical & Computer Engineering:
Sophomore Standing
Calculus for Engineers
Multivariable Calculus for Engineers

177

One of: Intro to Circuits for Elec. & Comp. Engineers (or Intro to Digital Logic Design *or* Signals & Information)
Intro to Computing using Java (or Intro to Computing using MATLAB)
Engineering General Chemistry I
Physics I: Mechanics
2 First-Year Writing Seminars

Junior Standing
Differential Equations for Engineers
Linear Algebra for Engineers
Two of: Intro to Circuits for Elec. & Comp. Engineers (or Intro to Digital Logic Design *or* Signals & Information)
Physics II: Heat/Electromagnetism
Physics III: Optics, Waves, & Particles
2 Liberal Studies Courses

Engineering Physics:
Sophomore Standing
Calculus for Engineers
Multivariable Calculus for Engineers
Introduction to Computing Using Java
Engineering General Chemistry I
Physics I: Mechanics
ANY ENGRI COURSE
2 First-Year Writing Seminars

Junior Standing
Differential Equations for Engineers
Linear Algebra for Engineers
Electronic Circuits (recommended)
Physics II: Heat/Electromagnetism
Physics III: Optics, Waves & Particles
2 Liberal Studies Courses

Environmental Engineering:
Sophomore Standing
Calculus for Engineers
Multivariable Calculus for Engineers
Intro to Computing Using JAVA (or Intro to Computer
Programming)
Engineering General Chemistry I
Intro to Organic & Biological Chemistry
Physics I: Mechanics
2 First-Year Writing Seminars

Junior Standing
Differential Equations for Engineers
Linear Algebra for Engineers
Mechanics of Solids
Physics II: Heat/Electromagnetism
2 Liberal Studies Courses
Biology Principles or Biological Sciences, Lectures & Biological
Sciences, Laboratory
One of (Engineering Thermodynamics; Engineering for a Sustainable
Society; Engineering Computation)

Material Science and Engineering:
Sophomore Standing
Calculus for Engineers
Multivariable Calculus for Engineers
Introduction to Computing Using Java
Engineering General Chemistry I
Mechanical Properties of Materials: from Nanodevices to
Superstructures (or Elec. Materials for the Info Age)
Physics I: Mechanics
2 First-Year Writing Seminars

Junior Standing
Differential Equations for Engineers
Linear Algebra for Engineers

179

Mechanical Properties of Materials: from Nanodevices to Superstructures
Elec. Materials for the Information Age
Atomic and Molecular Structure of Matter
Physics II: Heat/Electromagnetism
Physics III: Optics, Waves & Particles
2 Liberal Studies Courses

Information Science, Systems, and Technology:
*Note: If a student fails to satisfy Differential Equations for Engineers, then student must take Physics III: Optics, Waves & Particles instead of General Chemistry II.

Sophomore Standing
Calculus for Engineers
Multivariable Calculus for Engineers
Introduction to Computing Using Java
Intermediate Design & Programming for the Web
Physics I: Mechanics
2 First-Year Writing Seminars

Junior Standing
Linear Algebra for Engineers
Differential Equations for Engineers (or one of: Prove it!; Discrete Structures)
Object-Oriented Programming & Data Structures
Engineering Probability & Statistics
Physics II: Heat/Electromagnetism
Physics III: Optics, Waves & Particles
Data-Driven Web Applications
2 Liberal Studies Courses

Mechanical Engineering:
Note: Students may take Physics III: Optics, Waves & Particles or Intro to Circuits for Elec. & Comp. Engrs, if they cannot enroll in Mechanical Properties & Selection of Engineering Materials.

Calculus for Engineers
Multivariable Calculus for Engineers
Introduction to Computing Using Java
Engineering General Chemistry I
Physics I: Mechanics
2 First-Year Writing Seminars

Junior Standing
Differential Equations for Engineers
Linear Algebra for Engineers
Mechanics of Solids
Dynamics
Engineering Thermodynamics
Physics II: Heat/Electromagnetism
Mechanical Properties & Selection of Engineering Materials
Mechanical Synthesis
2 Liberal Studies Courses

Operations Research & Engineering:
Sophomore Standing
Calculus for Engineers
Multivariable Calculus for Engineers
Intro to Computing Using Java (or Intro to Computing - MATLAB)
Engineering General Chemistry I
Physics I: Mechanics
2 First-Year Writing Seminars

Junior Standing
Linear Algebra for Engineers
Differential Equations for Engineers (or one of the following: Prove it; Discrete Structures)
Object-Oriented Programming & Data Structures
Engineering Probability & Statistics
Physics II: Heat/Electromagnetism
Physics III: Optics, Waves & Particles

2 Liberal Studies Courses

Science of Earth Systems:
Sophomore Standing
Calculus for Engineers
Multivariable Calculus for Engineers
Introduction to Computing Using Java
Engineering General Chemistry I
Physics I: Mechanics
2 First Year Writing Seminars

Junior Standing
Differential Equations for Engineers
Linear Algebra for Engineers
Engineering General Chemistry I
Intro to Organic & Biological Chemistry
Physics II: Heat/Electromagnetism
Biology Principles
2 Liberal Studies Courses

Competitive Applicants:
Minimum B+/A- GPA (No Grades of C or Lower)

Cornell University:
School of Arts & Sciences

Address:
AS Admissions, 147 Goldwin Smith Hall, Ithaca, NY

Contact:
Admissions Director

Phone:
(607) 255-4833

Tuition:
NY Resident: $43,185 (2012-13)
Non-Resident: $43,185 (2012-13)

Interview Required:
No [Not offered]

Enrollment:
Fall, Spring

Admission Deadline:
March 1st – Fall
Oct. 1st – Spring

SAT Required:
Not Required

Required Coursework:
Must complete pre-requisites for major.
Note: If the student wants credit to transfer, the course must be equivalent to another course offered within the College of Arts & Sciences.

Students should not take:
Developmental or Remedial classes (reading or study skills); Practical or Skill-Oriented classes (e.g., word processing); Orientation; Teaching Assistantships; High-School Level Courses (e.g., pre-calc, college-prep); Physical Education; Military Science; Internship; EMT

Cornell University:
School of Agriculture & Life Sciences

Address:
CALS Admissions, 177 Roberts Hall, Ithaca, NY 14853

Contact:
Admissions Director

Phone:
(607) 255-2036

Tuition:
NY Resident: $23,310 (2012-13)
Non-Resident: $39,450 (2012-13)

Interview Required:
No [Not offered]

Enrollment:
Fall, Spring
Landscape Arch. [Fall Only]

Admission Deadline:
March 1st – Fall
Sept. - Oct. 1st – Spring

SAT Required:
Not Required

Required Coursework:
Check Course Sites for Required Breakdowns per Major

Cornell University:
School of Architecture, Art, & Planning

Address:
CAAP Admissions, 129 Sibley Dome, Ithaca, NY 14853

Contact:
Admissions Director

Phone:
(607) 255-2036

Tuition:
NY Resident: $39,450 (2012-13)
Non-Resident: $39,450 (2012-13)

Interview Required:
Yes [Architecture]

Enrollment:
Fall, Spring

Admission Deadline:
March 1st – Fall
Oct. 1st – Spring

SAT Required:
Not Required

Enrollment Exception: *Five-year Architecture* – Fall only, unless student completed two years in an accredited architecture program

Required Coursework:
Check Course Sites for Required Breakdowns per Major

Dartmouth College

Contact:

Ellen.D.Parish@ dartmouth.edu

Tel: (603) 646-1216

Fax: (603) 646-2875

Address:

Undergraduate Admissions

6016 McNutt Hall

Hanover, NH 03755

Application Fee: $80 or fee waiver

Application Packet: Common Application

Supplemental Packet: Required

Mid-Term Report: Not Required

College Transcripts: Required

High School Transcripts: Required

SAT/ACT: Required (Waivers Provided)

SAT II: Required (Waivers Provided)

AP, IB, or A Level Exams: Not Required [Unless Already Taken]

College(s):
Dartmouth College

Dartmouth College

Address:
Dartmouth College, Office of Undergraduate Admissions
6016 McNutt Hall, Hanover, NH 03755

Contact:
Senior Associate
Director of Admissions
Ellen D. Parish

Phone:
(603) 646-1216

Interview Required:
No [Not available]

Tuition:
$43,782 (2012-2013)

Admission Deadline:
March 1st – Fall

Enrollment:
Fall

Competitive GPA:
Not Reported

SAT/ACT:
1) SAT & 2 SAT Subject Tests *or* 2) ACT
-   Waiver available upon request if tests not yet taken

Preferred Coursework:
Not Reported

Required Coursework:
Not Reported

Requirements:
Take coursework at schools other than community colleges to ensure transfer of credit because Dartmouth will not accept credits from a community college.

Harvard University

Contact:

adm-tran@ fas.harvard.edu

Tel: (617) 495- 1551

Fax: (617) 495-8821

Address:

Harvard University

Transfer Admissions

86 Battle Street

Cambridge, MA 02138

Application Fee: $75 or fee waiver

Application Packet: Common Application

Supplemental Packet: Required

Mid-Term Report: Required

College Transcripts: Required

High School Transcripts: Required

SAT/ACT: Required

AP, IB, or A Level Exams: Not Required [Unless Already Taken]

College(s):
Harvard College

Harvard University

Address:
Committee on Transfer Admission
86 Battle Street, Cambridge, MA 02138

Contact:
Admissions Director

Phone:
(617) 495-1551

Tuition:
$37, 576 (2012-2013)

Interview Required:
No [Not available]

Enrollment:
Fall

Admission Deadline:
March 1st – Fall

SAT/ACT Required:
Yes
SAT II [Optional]

Competitive GPA:
Not Reported

Preferred Coursework:
Liberal Arts *[Heavy Emphasis]*

Required Coursework:
Not Reported

Requirements:
1 year collegiate study
Not more than 2 years collegiate study
No Vocational, Professional, Technical Courses
- Journalism, Business, Law, Nursing

Princeton University

Contact:

uaoffice@ princeton.edu

Tel: (609) 258-3060

Fax: (609)258-6743

Address:

Undergraduate Admissions

110 West College

P.O. Box 430

Princeton, NJ 08542-0430

Application Fee: N/A

Application Packet: No Application Packet Available

Supplemental Packet: Not Reported

Mid-Term Report: Not Reported

College Transcripts: Not Reported

High School Transcripts: Not Reported

SAT/ACT: Not Reported

AP, IB, or A Level Exams: Not Reported

College(s):
Princeton College

NOTE: Princeton University Does Not Currently Allow Transfer Admission.

Princeton University

Address:
Princeton University, Undergraduate Admission Office
110 West College, P.O. Box 430, Princeton, NJ 08542-0430

Contact:
Director of Admissions

Phone:
(609) 258-3060

Tuition:
$38,650 (2012-2013)

Interview Required:
No [Not available]

SAT/ACT:
Not Reported

Admission Deadline:
Not Reported

Enrollment:
Not Reported

Competitive GPA:
Not Reported

Preferred Coursework:
Not Reported

Required Coursework:
Not Reported

*Princeton could change their decision to admit transfers at any time.

University of Pennsylvania

Contact:

info@ admissions.upenn.edu

Tel: (215) 898-7507

Fax: (215) 898-9670

Address:

Undergraduate Admissions

1 College Hall, Room 1

Philadelphia, PA 19104

Application Fee: $80 or fee waiver

Application Packet: Common Application

Supplemental Packet: Required

Mid-Term Report: Required

College Transcripts: Required

High School Transcripts: Required

SAT/ACT: Required (Waivers Provided)

SAT II: Required (Waivers Provided)

AP, IB, or A Level Exams: Not Required [Unless Already Taken]

College(s):
College of Arts & Sciences
School of Engineering & Applied Science
School of Nursing
Wharton School
College of Liberal & Professional Studies

University of Pennsylvania: College of Arts & Sciences

Address:
120 Logan Hall, 249 S. 36th Street, Philadelphia, PA 19104

Contact:
Admissions Counselor

Phone:
(215) 898-6341

Tuition:
$37,620 (2012-2013)

Interview Required:
No [Not available]

Enrollment:
Fall

Admission Deadline:
March 15th

SAT/ACT:
Required

Competitive GPA:
Not Reported

Requirements:
Student records must be free of failure, conditional, and incomplete grades. If student took a class on a pass/fail or credit/no credit basis, grades or written evaluations must be sent by those professors.
- At least one full year of academic coursework (i.e., 8 classes)
- Major specific requirements are on Penn's website

Preferred Coursework:
Students should take courses geared toward, "... five foundational skills through writing, foreign language, quantitative data analysis, formal reasoning, and cross-cultural analysis; and seven sector requirements in society, history & tradition, arts & letters, the living world, the physical world, and two interdisciplinary sectors: humanities & social sciences and natural sciences & mathematics" (quoting The University of Pennsylvania's website).

University of Pennsylvania: School of Engineering & Applied Science

Address:
220 South 33rd Street, 107 Towne Building
Philadelphia, PA 19104-63911

Contact:
Admissions Counselor

Phone:
(215) 898-7246

Tuition:
$37,620 (2012-2013)

Interview Required:
No [Not available]

Enrollment:
Fall

Admission Deadline:
March 15th – Fall

SAT/ACT:
Required

Competitive GPA:
Not Reported

Requirements:

After *one year of college*, students desiring to transfer into the school of Engineering & Applied Science should have completed at least:

- One course in Chemistry
- One course in Physics (involving the use of Calculus)
- One course in Computer Programming
- Two courses in Calculus, and,
- If possible, two courses in the Social Sciences and Humanities

Students pursuing a major in Bioengineering, Computer Engineering, Mechanical Engineering and Applied Mechanics, Materials Science and Engineering, Systems Science and Engineering, Electrical Engineering, and Market and Social Systems Engineering should also complete a second course in Physics.

After *two years of college*, students desiring to transfer into the School of Engineering and Applied Science should have completed at least:

- A total of four courses in math (Calculus through Differential Equations),
- Two courses in Physics (involving the use of Calculus),
- One course in Chemistry,
- One course in Computer Programming,
- Three or four courses in the Social Sciences and Humanities, and
- As many Engineering and Applied Science courses as possible (e.g., Mechanics, Electrical Circuits, Materials, Thermodynamics, etc.)

In addition, Computer Science, Computer Engineering, Digital Media Design, and Market and Social Systems Engineering students must take a second computer programming course.

University of Pennsylvania: School of Nursing

Address:
Claire M. Fagin Hall, 418 Curie Boulevard
Philadelphia, PA 19104-4217

Contact:
Admissions Counselor

Phone:
(215) 898-4271

Tuition:
$37,620 (2012-2013)

Interview Required:
Required

Enrollment:
Fall

Admission Deadline:
March 15th

SAT/ACT:
Required

Competitive GPA:
Not Reported

Requirements:
Transfer applicants must have completed a minimum of eight transferable college courses and the following prerequisite courses:

- Introductory to Chemistry I with lab
- Introduction to Biology I with lab
- Introduction to Anatomy and Physiology I and II with lab
- Introduction to Microbiology (only recommended)

Applicants with a Bachelor's degree in a non-nursing discipline, and applicants who are RN Return students (those who have completed a Diploma RN program or an Associate's Degree RN program) must apply to the Accelerated BSN 2nd Degree or BSN/MSN program.

University of Pennsylvania: Wharton School of Business

Address:
1 College Hall, Philadelphia, PA 19104-6376

Contact:
Admissions Counselor

Phone:
(215) 898-7507

Tuition:
$37,620 (2012-2013)

Interview Required:
No [Not available]

Enrollment:
Fall

Admission Deadline:
March 15th

SAT/ACT:
Required

Competitive GPA:
Not Reported

Requirements:
Applicants who desire admittance during sophomore year must have completed:
- One semester of Calculus, which can be fulfilled by:
  o A score of 5 on the AP Calculus BC exam;
  o A score of 7 on the IB Higher Level Mathematics with Further Mathematics exam; or
  o A course deemed to be equivalent to Math 104
- One semester of Introductory Micro-Economics, which can be fulfilled by:
  o A score of 5 on the AP Micro-Economics exam;
  o A score of 6 or 7 on the IB higher level Economics exam;
  o A course deemed to be equivalent to Econ 001

- One semester of Introductory Macro-Economics, which can be fulfilled by:
    o A score of 5 on the AP Micro-Economics exam;
    o A score of 6 or 7 on the IB higher level Economics exam;
    o A course deemed to be equivalent to Econ 002
- Or, in lieu of separate introductory courses in Micro and Macro-Economics,
    o One semester of a combined introductory Micro and Macro-Economics course (Econ 010), which can be fulfilled by a course equivalent to Econ 010.

In addition to the above requirements, applicants who desire admittance during junior year must have completed:
- One semester Financial Accounting course equivalent to ACCT 101
- One semester Managerial Accounting course equivalent to ACCT 102
- Two semesters of Statistics (with a Calculus prerequisite)
    o A score of "5" on the AP statistics exam will only fulfill the State 101 requirement.
- One semester of Intermediate Micro-Economics, which can be fulfilled by:
    o A course equivalent to ECON 101; or
    o A course equivalent to BPUB 250.

*Foreign language proficiency is recommended by the time an individual enrolls at The University of Pennsylvania. Proficiency is generally equal to four semesters of college-level language courses and must be demonstrated by passing a proficiency exam at The University of Pennsylvania before graduation.

University of Pennsylvania:
College of Liberal & Professional Studies

Address:
120 Logan Hall, 249 S. 36th Street, Philadelphia, PA 19104

Contact:
Admissions Counselor

Phone:
(215) 898-6341

Tuition:
$37,620 (2012-2013)

Interview Required:
No [Not available]

Enrollment:
Fall

Admission Deadline:
March 15th

SAT/ACT:
Required

Competitive GPA:
Not Reported

Requirements:
*The college of liberal and professional studies offers courses in the evening on a full or part-time basis.
*If you have been absent from formal study for a short while and are interested in part-time or full-time study in the evening, then you should apply to the College of Liberal and Professional Studies.

Note: Students who have been denied admission to any Bachelor's degree program at the University of Pennsylvania must wait one year before applying to the LPS Bachelor of Arts program.

Yale University

Contact:

trans.admissions@yale.edu

Tel: (203) 432-9300

Fax: (203) 432- 9370

Address:

Undergraduate Admissions

38 Hillhouse Avenue

New Haven, CT 06511

Application Fee: $75 or fee waiver

Application Packet: Common Application

Supplemental Packet: Required

Mid-Term Report: Required

College Transcripts: Required

High School Transcripts: Required

SAT/ACT: Required

AP, IB, or A Level Exams: Not Required [Unless Already Taken]

College(s):
Yale College

Yale University

Address:
Office of Undergraduate Admissions, P.O. Box 208234
New Haven, CT 06520-8234

Contact:
Admissions Director

Phone:
(203) 432-9300

Tuition:
$42,300 (2012-2013)

Interview Required:
No [Not offered]

Enrollment:
Fall Only

Admission Deadline:
March 1st – Fall

SAT/ACT Required:
Yes
SAT II [Optional]

Competitive GPA:
3.8 GPA

Course Credit:
Courses are evaluated individually

Preferred Coursework:
Liberal Arts Curriculum

Required Coursework:
Major Specific
-   "While most majors are open to transfer students, some departments have specific rules or prerequisites that prevent some transfer students from pursuing the major" (quoting Yale's Transfer Admission Website).

Requirements:
At least 1 year of collegiate study

Disclaimer

The resources and information set forth in this book may change yearly. This book is meant to be used as a guideline. Please double check the admissions websites for the Ivy League universities if you have a particular college or program in which you want to enroll. This book is not meant to be used as a substitute for standards set forth on the admissions office websites for each Ivy League institution. I will update information as I deem necessary on my website, which is www.transfereducation.com. Please check my website to see if any of the information set forth in this book has been updated. Although I provide you with an alternative approach for acquiring admittance into the nation's most sought after colleges and universities at the most cost effective price, I do not, and cannot, guarantee that you will attain admission into an Ivy League university or any other school for that matter. Nor, can I guarantee that you will save money in your endeavor. This disclaimer operates to indemnify me from any and all claims, suits and judgments that may arise out of the use of this literary work.

Made in the USA
Charleston, SC
16 May 2013